Praise for *Pivot for Success*

"Historically, the principles of rigid resolve and fierce intractability have been baked into the nation's DNA. Now comes Amy Hilliard with *Pivot for Success*, in which she draws on her own character-building personal and career experiences to convincingly reinforce the counterargument that, in today's fickle and fast-moving environment, the inability or unwillingness to pivot can easily lead to unfortunate and unfixable results. This book is based on the most solid kind of research: the kind derived from the real-life story of a highly accomplished, keen observer of human behavior. It says that we must all learn to dodge the curve balls that fate will invariably throw at us, and that life is not going to adjust itself to custom fit our master plan. This book supplants the sin of certitude with the positive power of pivotability."

—Tom Burrell,
Founder, Burrell Communications

"In *Pivot for Success*, Amy Hilliard provides a step-by-step guide of how to not only survive but thrive in corporate America. From defining priorities to having patience (my personal favorite!) she does a masterful job of sharing the lessons learned throughout her storied career."

—Mellody Hobson,
Co-CEO and President of Ariel Investments

"With bracing candor and boundless wit, Amy Hilliard's *Pivot for Success* offers inspiring stories of invention and reinvention drawn from her own remarkable life and career and provides concrete guidance about how to create a life of purpose and fulfillment by transforming difficulty into opportunity."

—Phylicia Rashad,
Actor/Director/Producer

"I love this book! Amy is one of the country's great thought leaders. She is also an excellent businesswoman with an abundance of diverse experiences. This book successfully melds those two attributes, thought leadership and realistic experiences, with the result being a pragmatic tool for success."

—Steven Rogers,
Harvard Business School, Senior Lecturer (Retired)

"Powerful, clear, dynamic, and impactful—these are just some of the reasons that make *this* book so important. It is based on true experiences and fortified with the knowledge gained from the life experiences, and it helps the many people Amy has mentored.

I have seen her apply each of the 10 Pivot Points and obtain extremely successful results over and over. I have literally followed Amy for years. As her sister, I assure you each chapter will give you a place to identify yourself and use and gain effective ways to steer your career and life in the direction of your dreams."

—**Gloria Mayfield Banks,**
#1 Worldwide Elite Executive National Sales Director—Mary Kay, Inc.;
International Success Strategist, CEO, Gloria Mayfield Banks, Inc.

"I've known Amy for 30+ years and witnessed her marketing acumen and brilliance firsthand at the Pillsbury Company. As much as I thought I knew about her journey, I learned so much more by reading her honest, no-holds-barred account of successfully overcoming adversity. For all who clamor for the keys to living richly, envision prosperity and dig in for a revealing read."

—**Jerri DeVard,**
C-Suite Executive and Corporate Board Director

"Whether we know it or not, we're all about to pivot—out of a year that has changed our lives and our world, forever. Whatever you're facing, with Amy Hilliard's *Pivot for Success*, you got this!"

—**Caroline Clarke**,
Founder and Former Chief Brand Officer, Black Enterprise Women of Power, SVP, Content Strategy & Thought Leadership, Nielsen Media

"Amy Hilliard has written a very good new book that essentially recalls ancient wisdom: vision, resilience, and perseverance matter still. Every generation faces the same problems in different settings. She reminds us that no matter the circumstances, personal character will ultimately determine one's ability to survive and thrive in spite of the challenges. This book allows us to follow her own journey, and I recommend it to you."

—**Carol Moseley Braun,**
U.S. Ambassador, U.S. Senator (Retired)

"*Pivot for Success* is a book that is so needed in these times and in this environment. As we all try to establish what's normal in today's world, Amy lays out several guidelines to get anyone back on track. This book will inspire you to push through your difficulties and refocus your efforts in a very strategic and tactical way that's also easy to understand."

—**Louis Carr,**
President of Media Sales at BET Networks

"Amy can talk about success because she has been extremely successful in many roles and businesses. This book couldn't be more timely. Being successful in this new world mandates the ability to 'Pivot!' This is the manual on how to do it."

—Charles Jenkins,
Filmmaker, Businessman, Multi-Award-Winning Songwriter/Artist

"I first met Amy over 10 years ago. Having both learned from and worked directly with Amy, I've been blessed to see her gift for inspiring others to push past what's possible up close. Her uncanny ability to genuinely connect with almost anyone has opened doors and broken down barriers, serving as a true testament to the validity of what she exhorts (or in other words, she most certainly practices what she preaches!).

I believe Amy's effectiveness comes from the fact that she truly lives the principles outlined in this book every day. Amy's approach brings practical and tangible steps for continuing to move forward. Both uplifting and challenging, *Pivot for Success* strikes a great balance of what we all need, similar to the qualities of a great coach. Throughout the book, Amy establishes a clear "why" for each step of her well-honed process, supported by both personal stories and valuable anecdotes from the amazing 'Who's Who' of her personal network.

Given our current context, this book and its insights could not be more relevant. If "unprecedented" has become the universal condition for the world in which we live, 'pivot' absolutely should be the universal remedy we all adopt."

—Karla Davis,
Vice President, Integrated Marketing & Media of ULTA Beauty,
friend and mentee

"From corporate leader to entrepreneur, Amy Hilliard delivers a compelling framework for 'believing in your possibilities,' and showcasing why 'pivots create purpose.'"

—Bonita C. Stewart,
VP, Global Partnerships, Google; coauthor, *A Blessing: Women of Color Teaming Up to Lead, Empower, and Thrive*

"Amy S. Hilliard has been an agent of change throughout her career. After a year like 2020, this book could not be better timed. *Pivot for Success* is a roadmap that can be your guidepost to success, no matter where you are in life or your career. Follow the 10 Pivot Points and manifest your success . . . Bravo, Amy."

—Brenda Lauderback,
Chairman, Denny's Corporation; Past President, Nine West
Footwear Group

"Amy has had a fascinating career as an intrapreneur, entrepreneur, and a pioneer in diversity marketing. She has leveraged her skills to inspire and innovate, and in this book, she provides insightful guidance on how anyone can navigate the successes and challenges of your career and personal life."

—**Linda Darragh,**
The Larry Levy Executive Director and Clinical Professor, Kellogg Innovation and Entrepreneurship Initiative, Kellogg Business School

"Amy is a gifted storyteller and so very relatable. One might read the title and say, 'Oh my goodness, not another book about pivoting,' and yes, in these tough times of a once-in-a-generation pandemic and economic collapse, pivoting is what we must do. But this is a story that goes beyond that; it is a quintessential American story told through the eyes and heart of a Black woman entrepreneur from Detroit whose words leap out at you and hold your hand as a guide, navigating you through your own personal journey to success. I thought I had heard and seen all the business advice/motivation one needs in a lifetime, but this is truly a unique approach to success, self-realization, and personal revelation. I strongly endorse Amy S. Hilliard's *Pivot for Success*."

—**Terrez Marriott Thompson,**
Retired, Coca-Cola, VP Global Supplier Diversity Founder and Chair, Powered By Zerret, Incorporated

PIVOT FOR SUCCESS

AMY S. HILLIARD

PIVOT

FOR

SUCCESS

Hone Your Vision,
Shift Your Energy,
Make Your Move

WILEY

Published by John Wiley & Sons, Inc., Hoboken, New Jersey.
Published simultaneously in Canada.

For general information on our other products and services or for technical support, please contact our Customer Care Department within the United States at (800) 762-2974, outside the United States at (317) 572-3993 or fax (317) 572-4002.

Wiley publishes in a variety of print and electronic formats and by print-on-demand. Some material included with standard print versions of this book may not be included in e-books or in print-on-demand. If this book refers to media such as a CD or DVD that is not included in the version you purchased, you may download this material at http://booksupport.wiley.com. For more information about Wiley products, visit www.wiley.com.

Library of Congress Cataloging-in-Publication Data is Available:

ISBN 978-1-119-78097-7 (Hardback)
ISBN 978-1-119-78099-1 (ePDF)
ISBN 978-1-119-78098-4 (ePub)

COVER DESIGN: PAUL MCCARTHY

SKY10026724_043021

This book is dedicated to my parents,
Stratford and Gwendolyn Hilliard,
whose strong spirits still guide me every single day.
And to my children,
Angelica and Nicholas Jones,
who light my life with their love and support always.

Contents

Introduction

AT THE END of 2013, I was sitting in the office of The Comfort-Cake® Company, the dream business I started in 2001 that sold pound cakes based on my recipes to United Airlines, Walmart, Home Shopping Network, the Chicago Public Schools (CPS), and several grocery chains across the country. I had just ended a call with my lawyer, who had laid out my options for holding on to the business. It had been a very difficult few years. We had started out strong, won awards, and even became an approved supplier to McDonald's. Yet several events had taken their toll on the business and on my finances: the recession of 2008; the decision by CPS to take desserts off the school menus; the need to switch to other offerings; and my desire to help care for my ailing dad. As I looked at the paperwork before me, I made up my mind: I would declare personal bankruptcy so that the business would survive. And it did. Doing so was one of the hardest decisions I've ever had to make, and no one but my family and closest friends even knew about it. For years, I just wasn't ready or able to tell my full story—until now.

I'm a Harvard MBA, a successful senior corporate executive, and a serial entrepreneur whose journey has been different from what you may expect. The things that happened to me weren't in anybody's textbook, nor were they what I or anyone could have predicted would happen. I've made it to senior levels of corporate America, been profiled by national publications, honored by the US Department of Commerce—and been bankrupted, foreclosed on, laid off, and divorced twice. Yet I'm here to share that even when you think you've lost it all, you can actually win everything. I'm here to share lessons learned from a life of dreams realized, and dreams deferred—lessons of how to keep it moving through the landscapes of success, failure, triumph, and tragedy. Most of all, I'm here to share the reason I'm still standing tall: I know how to **Pivot** and I learned when to make the turn.

In these pages, I will share with you how to Hone Your Vision, Shift Your Energy, and Make Your Move. In today's times, if you aren't willing to change, you will be left behind. One thing we all know for sure is that Life. Will. Change. And you must be able to change with it. It can be hard, but don't be afraid to Reinvent yourself and build the Resilience it takes to do it. In doing so, you may find Resurrection as you grow. Listen—Jesus isn't the only one who has risen from the dead! Dreams, plans, businesses, and more can come alive again if you learn how to Pivot. Over the years, I've developed a simple system and a strategic process that has worked for me, and I have been guided to share it with you.

It does not matter if you are an aspiring professional, at the beginning of your career, at the midpoint, or in the third act of your career and life. If you are looking to make some changes, you may feel stuck or overwhelmed by the challenges. My goal for *Pivot for Success* is to provide an easy-to-use framework to make those changes; based on that framework, I share stories from my life of how you can use my 10 Pivot Points strategically to make the changes you need. As I complete this book at the very beginning of 2021, we are in an incredible period of disruption, and also a time when history is being made. We all need to rise and use our gifts to bring positive energy to the world. This is not a time to be afraid. Why? The pace of change is so fast that if you are afraid of uncertainty and don't move forward, you will become obsolete.

It's time to get comfortable with being uncomfortable. Now is not the time to stick our heads in the sand and wish for the best. Nor is it a time for just protest. Although protest is vitally important, we need concrete action on many levels to make the moves that get the results the world needs now. With Reinvention, Resilience, and Resurrection, our mindsets can motivate us forward toward lives we never could have dreamed of, or thought were out of reach, especially when the world is turned upside down.

Entrepreneurship Is in My DNA

I grew up in Detroit and always wanted to please my parents, who had high expectations for me and my three sisters. We were expected to get good grades, be good girls, marry, and have a family. Entrepreneurship was okay as a side hustle—both my parents did that. But full time? That wasn't really embraced. Getting a good J-O-B was the right thing to do. But I always heard the whisper of my own siren song, so I tried many things, balancing bouts of doubt with fearless actions. *Pivot for Success* tells what I went through to land a debate team scholarship to go to my dream school, Howard University in Washington, DC, when I already had a full scholarship to go to Michigan State. I didn't realize it then, but entrepreneurship was in my DNA. As a kid, I took rose petals from my mother's prized rose garden, soaked them in water, filled little vials, and sold "perfume" to my mother's friends. The fragrance of being my own boss was compelling, seductive, and addictive. At 10 or 11, I had a lock on babysitting in my neighborhood. Later on, even when I worked for someone else, I was an intrapreneur, always wanting to create something new or do things my own way.

At the age of 48, I started The ComfortCake Company, makers of "Pound Cake So Good It Feels Like a Hug." Yet, even armed with an Ivy League degree and more than 20 years of corporate experience during which my teams successfully launched multimillion-dollar brands, banks wouldn't give me a loan. No matter. I pivoted, sold my home to finance the business, and United Airlines became our first customer.

Another Pivot occurred when my favorite cousin was killed in a tragic car accident and I had to comb a wig on her head while the mortician put her face back together. In that moment I came to a profound understanding about life. I knew then that as long as I wasn't dead, if I could look up, I could get up. These and many other stories have built my Resilience, ignited Reinvention, and helped me embrace Resurrection in many forms.

This book covers the 10 Pivot Points, or Power Ps, as I originally called them, that have guided me for decades as I've made key decisions. I initially presented the Power Ps in my first guidebook, *Tap Into Your Juice*, in 2005. I'm deeply honored that Michelle Obama endorsed these Powers Ps and my guidebook, and after she became First Lady, she gave me her endorsement of them *for life*. The Power Ps are now my 10 Pivot Points and are part of a 3-Step Strategic Pivot Process that has helped me stay on my path. The great thing about them is that they are flexible and interchangeable for the evolving decisions and life stages that happen.

I've been using the Pivot Points since 1997, giving seminars, following the guidebook, and speaking about them, and will continue to do so. When I recently went to my storage unit to look for some notes, I realized just how long it's taken to get this full book written—23 years! It also shows how thoroughly I've integrated the 10 Pivot Points into my life, both professionally and personally.

The 10 Pivot Points are simple to remember, easy to use, and are universal. They never go out of style. I have taught them worldwide and have dusted them off to apply them relentlessly to myself to know which way to turn. I still do. There's an old Latin proverb that says, "By learning you will teach; by teaching you will learn." Well, Amen to that!

Pivot for Success is divided into 10 chapters, one for each of the Pivot Points I live by.

Pivot Point #1: *Finding Your Purpose*—What gift is uniquely yours, like a fingerprint, that you can share to help others?

Pivot Point #2: *Believing in Possibilities*—What's possible now? A year from now? Five years from now? Who can help you?

Pivot Point #3: *Defining Your Priorities*—If you knew you had five years left to live what would you be doing? Three years? One year? Why aren't you doing that *now*?

Pivot Point #4: *Envisioning Prosperity*—Prosperity isn't always about money, and all money isn't green.

Pivot Point #5: *Getting Prepared*—Like the company Dream-Works®, you have to work to live your dreams.

Pivot Point #6: *Having Patience*—Putting one foot in front of the other is the only way to create a path.

Pivot Point #7: *Seeking Positivity*—Positive thoughts and people are necessities, not luxuries.

Pivot Point #8: *Honoring Your Passion*—It's the lubricant that keeps your dreams alive.

Pivot Point #9: *Maintaining Perseverance*—Developing "bounce-backability" is imperative.

Pivot Point #10: *Managing Perceptions*—There's no such thing as a second first impression, yet don't advertise what you don't have.

When making decisions and considering which Pivot Points best fit your situation, the 3-Step Strategic Pivot Process will help you keep focus on your decisions. You'll see in the book which Pivot Points are recommended under which step and how they align with where you are in the process:

1. Hone Your Vision—About the Decision
2. Shift Your Energy—To Meet the Decision
3. Make Your Move—Toward the Decision

That's how I've done it. Grounded in faith, and using these tools, I've been able to keep it moving. By sharing these tools I've helped others. Nothing gives me more gratification than knowing that my stories of success, struggle, failure, and sustainability have helped thousands of people see that they can make it, too. The stories I share about my life and experiences represent various perspectives about what it takes to make it in business and in life. Few people have created multimillion-dollar brands in senior corporate positions, legendary entrepreneurial environments, and start-ups. Not to mention, few have done it as a woman, and as a woman of color. I want to share my journey as you move forward on yours! Here's some of what I'll let you in on:

- How growing up in Detroit, among hard-working people, entrepreneurs, and creative geniuses ignited my dreams. And how witnessing the impact of segregation and integration fueled my determination.
- How getting into and studying at Howard University fundamentally changed my worldview of who I could become and what my value could be in the world.
- How pivoting my ambitions to higher levels got me into Harvard Business School, a buying position at a major retail store, access to the fashion houses of New York City, and senior executive positions in corporate America and legendary entrepreneurial firms.
- What happened when I had to pivot from my ambitions and be true to the traditions of family that called my spirit.
- Knowing that entrepreneurship was in my blood, how I pivoted to build a pathway into that world.
- What happened when I turned full-time into entrepreneurship, and the many pivots necessary to create and sustain more than one business.
- How I kept pivoting when failure closed doors and opportunity opened others.

As I write this introduction at my dining room table with notes and books surrounding me, I'm reminded of seeing my mom, when I was in grade school, write her master's thesis at our dining room table on my grandfather's manual typewriter. Books and notes everywhere, carbon paper nearby. I feel her spirit cheering me on. It is my sincere hope that my experiences and circumstances may spark a solution to some of the challenges and opportunities you face and that by following these solutions, you too can learn to *Pivot for Success* and *Hone Your Vison, Shift Your Energy,* and *Make Your Move.*

I look forward to joining you on your journey!

Amy S. Hilliard
January 3, 2021

Part I: Hone Your Vision

1

Finding Your Purpose

Just as your fingerprints leave a unique mark, so does the gift of your purpose.

WHENEVER I'VE GIVEN a speech, and people come up to me afterwards to thank me for inspiring them to pursue their dream of starting a business or make a strategic move, it gives me a feeling of deep satisfaction. The same is true when I've helped someone with a career decision or business issue. Marketing is my expertise; I have decades of professional experience and I've taught marketing at the university level. Inspiring others is like teaching. When the lightbulb comes on in a student's eyes, and they "get it," their excitement becomes real. Suddenly, a pathway, an example of something I showed them, or how I did it has opened the door for them and, boy, that's exciting!

The same feeling sweeps over me when it comes to helping others maintain a healthy lifestyle as we age. When I turned 60, I created a blog—*Sizzling After 60*—to chronicle my journey to thrive at every stage of life; I present my journey as a blueprint for others to follow. Over the years, I've realized that inspiring others is my purpose. In a way, it is my ministry. It is what people come to me for and have for years. It makes me feel *good* that others are able to move forward positively thanks to what I've been able to share with them. It's my unique fingerprint, and I believe that in its own way, it helps the world. #inspiringothers

Finding Your Purpose Can Serve Others and Move Mountains

That's what Finding Your Purpose can do. We all have a purpose—that unique gift that we can each share with others to positively help a business, your community, and the world. For example, the COVID-19 pandemic moved the world into a new normal. As such, many of us had to make significant changes in our lives—often suddenly and unplanned. In doing so, Finding Your Purpose and using it may have had to fall by the wayside as bills needed to be paid. I urge you, however, not to discount the power of purpose in challenging times. It is what we *all* are gifted to do. Finding Your Purpose is listed as the first Pivot Point because I believe that operating from a sense of purpose can be the foundation for so much of what you do in life.

As I shared in my book *Tap Into Your Juice*, nature provides some wonderful examples of purposeful existence. Everything in nature has a purpose. Birds fly, flowers grow, and the sun can't help but shine. They each do what they are meant to do. It's the same with us, when we discover our purpose. I love how purpose is often described: purpose is the reason something or someone exists. It can also be how something is used or made—which leads to an intended goal or result. Once you discover what your gifts are, you can pivot toward endeavors that use them with determination and resoluteness in your life choices and in service for others. I've found that serving others provides important balance with your values. Finding

Your Purpose and using it in your daily life is great for your health, reduces stress, and is an amazing personal superpower! When you use it, particularly in challenging times, you'll find motivation when you need it and the ability to Hone Your Vision, Shift Your Energy, and Make Your Move.

What's interesting for me is that inspiring others doesn't mean that I'm always sharing stories of triumph or of "knowing it all." Not by a long shot. In 1986, when I was a relatively new product manager at Gillette, I was given the job of managing two of the oldest brands in the Personal Care Division, Adorn and White Rain Hairsprays. I guess they figured I couldn't mess up those highly profitable brands—just keep shipping them, right? Well, obviously this was before the days of social media, and I was getting about 10 letters a week from customers who remembered the old White Rain Shampoo that Gillette marketed in the 1950s and 60s. I couldn't believe it. I figured if that many people were taking the time to write to ask a company to bring back a product, *lots* of customers might want it to come to back. Gillette had tried a "new and improved" version of White Rain Shampoo in the 1970s; it was fruit scented in various colors and didn't do well. These customers wanted the original, crystal-clear version back. So, I had to inspire my management to let me bring back this product. It was a process, and I needed to draw on my Purpose to carry it out.

Using your Purpose can be spontaneous and it can also be strategic, or a combination of both. I used a combined strategic and spontaneous inspirational approach I call "Hallway Management" for gaining approval to relaunch White Rain Shampoo at Gillette. What's that, you may ask? Well, whenever I saw my boss, the VP, or the president of the division at the water cooler in the hall, I'd tell them about *all* the letters I received asking to bring back the original White Rain Shampoo. It was a casual, excited, but determined and purposeful way of inspiring them to see the potential in bringing back that product. Finally, after several hallway encounters and additional mentions in more formal meetings, I was given the green light. I was told I could launch the product with the following parameters: I had a six-month timetable and no increase in my budget. I had inspired a "yes." Next, I had to inspire the team to make it happen.

I had assisted on new product launches at Gillette while climbing the ladder, but those were well supported with major budgets and long planning times. This was very different—I was now the project lead with a super short planning window. I knew it was a major career risk, and we had to make it a success. Knowing I had to light others up with the idea, I called a meeting of everyone who would be involved to jump-start the project—Manufacturing, R&D, Packaging, Sales, Market Research, Advertising, and Art Design. When we were all in the room, I told them, "Congratulations! I've been getting a ton of letters from customers asking to bring back the clear White Rain Shampoo. Management has just given us the green light to relaunch it! I'm not sure how to do it. But I know *you all do*. I want to hear from each of your areas how we can do it fast and profitably. We only have six months to get it out the door on and on the shelves. So, let's get started!"

The team sat in stunned silence at first. Marketing had never called a new products meeting like that before. Usually, Marketing came to the subject matter experts with a concept fully planned out, and their job was to execute it. They were not in on the initial planning stages. Well, let me tell you. Within minutes, that team came forth with incredible ideas. "We have a shampoo bottle that works with the line that's already tooled, and production line approved," said Manufacturing. "We have a wonderful clear shampoo formula and fragrance that beats Suave, and has been sitting on the shelf for a while," said R&D. "We can turn the hair spray graphics into shampoo graphics that will fit that bottle," said Art Design and Packaging after they huddled together. "I think we can do a tag on our regional advertising media flight," Advertising chimed in and Market Research agreed they'd look into that also. After a while, I had to slow everyone down so my assistant product manager and

I could capture all the notes! It was just amazing and taught me very valuable lessons about Finding Your Purpose and using it. I knew I could inspire people, but respecting others, being transparent, vulnerable, and authentic in the process is what can galvanize and motivate people to take action. Being perfect is not important. Being real is.

White Rain Shampoo was relaunched in six months with much success and went on to help grow the White Rain franchise from $25 million to a $100 million business. I was asked to write up the launch process we used. The New Products Development process at Gillette was changed: starting with bringing the subject expert teams together at the beginning of the process instead of much later on. In addition, the work of my team to get this done was chronicled in a case study for the Darden School of Business at the University of Virginia.

My 10 years at Gillette were a pivotal time for me and provided incredible opportunities to use Finding My Purpose as I developed in my assignments there. I say this because people often think that you need to be working in your purpose as the total sum of your job or career. For some, that is possible. But as long as you can use your purpose consistently within your endeavors, it can still provide major satisfaction, and steer you as you pivot forward. This worked for me at Gillette.

Coming from Detroit I saw Black entrepreneurs all around me—all with Purpose—including Berry Gordy, who built the Motown music empire within walking distance of my home. I grew up with a profound respect for Black entrepreneurship and Black representation in business. I saw firsthand what it took to be successful, including watching the Supremes in green sequined evening gowns singing their No. 1 hit at the Michigan State Fair while the pigs oinked loudly in the background. Nothing stopped them! As a teenager I saw my mother cut up her Saks Fifth Avenue credit card (I begged her not to do it) and send it with a letter to the President of Saks saying she would no longer shop there until they put Black models in their catalog—and he wrote her back saying they would! So, when I got to Gillette and saw that there was no advertising in Black magazines like *Ebony*, *Jet*, and *Essence*, I decided I would raise the question as to why not every chance I respectfully could. I brought it up in meetings with management and the advertising agencies. I would ask, "We use shampoo, hairspray, and deodorant. These magazines reach millions of consumers and they have billions of dollars to spend. Why aren't we going after their business?" My goal for using my Purpose of inspiring others was clear and strategic. Over time, Gillette's Personal Care Division started advertising in Black magazines on a regular basis. I was deeply satisfied when the cofounder of *Essence* magazine thanked me personally for one of the ad spreads from Gillette that helped him during a challenging time for his business.

This advocacy led me to a career pivot I never envisioned. By Finding and using my Purpose to inspire others, I was instrumental in helping Gillette recognize that the Black hair care market was exploding, and they didn't have a piece of it. A couple of years later, they asked me to be a part of the acquisition team to acquire a Black hair care company. Although I took a finance course at Harvard Business School and liked it, I was not schooled in acquisitions. But the next thing I knew, I was flying all over the country asking the premier owners of Black hair care companies if they wanted to sell to Gillette. In many cases, it was just me. And them. Over lunch or in meetings in their offices. Or in one case, at the Lustrasilk Corporation, over dinner with the owners, and then during a tour of their state-of-the-art manufacturing plant while it was closed so the employees would not know of our discussions.

It was a heady time, working with my mentor and boss, Linda Keene, on the team when Gillette ultimately acquired the Lustrasilk Corporation. Interestingly, Lustrasilk was never owned by Black entrepreneurs, but by a German former piano salesman and a Mexican former chemist from 3M who developed a product that would straighten sheep's hair. They figured there were a lot of people in the world with woolly type hair and built a $50 million business on that idea with products to service them. From my work on that project, I was promoted to Director of Marketing for Lustrasilk and moved with my family to Minneapolis.

While the Lustrasilk plant was state of the art, the bookkeeping and sales data were not. The books were kept by hand, as was the sales data. I literally spent weeks inputting sales data unit by unit into a computer so I could track trends and begin making future plans. In the meantime, Gillette was pressing for new products to boost sales. There was no brand management team, just the loyal team at Lustrasilk. We had to move fast to get things going with new products. Based on what I learned from the White Rain Shampoo experience, I leveraged Finding My Purpose and called a meeting with all the subject matter experts and asked them what we could launch quickly. A similar process happened. The head of R&D had a product he was convinced would beat the most popular oil moisturizer on the market. He'd been working on it for years, but the owners didn't see it as a priority. The manufacturing and packaging teams could produce it with no problems. I came up with a name on a flight back from Boston and legal cleared it. The advertising agency knew the power of radio and came up with a brilliant creative strategy to drive distribution. The *team* was inspired to make it happen and happen it did. When the radio ads broke all over the country, they were so successful that consumers were in stores begging for "Moisture Max." We met our sales and distribution goals, and Gillette was pleased. I was super proud of the Lustrasilk team and, importantly, they were proud of themselves. Finding and using my Purpose was a unique way of inspiring others, and it was transferable. It was another important lesson. Fingerprints are indelible— something else to remember.

Align Your Purpose with Your Values and What You Enjoy

Another thing to keep in mind is that sometimes the gift of your Purpose may not always work as you expect. Even when you have Found Your Purpose, the timing and circumstances for using it needs to align.

As time went on at Lustrasilk, Gillette decided to close the Lustrasilk plant and move production to a nearby large plant they owned in St. Paul, Minnesota. I was against this move, as it would eliminate a key factor in Lustrasilk's success—just-in-time manufacturing. Gillette's large systems required six-month lead times. The sales team and I at Lustrasilk could literally ask the VP of manufacturing to close down line 7 and bring up line 11 to produce a big order that came in that day. The plant move meant all that flexibility would go away. Well, the president of Lustrasilk, the VP of sales, and I—all Black and Gillette veterans—got together and decided we were going to buy Lustrasilk. Now, part of my Purpose worked, as I was able to inspire venture capitalists to raise $75 million to buy Lustrasilk. But I couldn't inspire Gillette to sell. We tried *hard*. They said no and decided to move all other company operations to Boston. Closing the Lustrasilk plant was one of the hardest professional things I've ever had to participate in. Those people gave their hearts and souls to make the company work, and I had to hand them a "Thank You" mug and shake their hands good-bye. As I did not want to return to Boston, I made the decision to leave Gillette and look for another career move.

My sister, Gloria Mayfield Banks, was just starting her career with Mary Kay Cosmetics around this time in 1989. She recruited everyone in the family who could walk, talk, and chew gum to become a consultant on her team. She is now, by the way, the #1 Executive Elite National Sales Director for all of Mary Kay Cosmetics. But I digress. I had a severance package from Gillette and had enjoyed sales while I was there, so I decided to give Mary Kay a try. I was in fact considering sales as a next move because I really enjoyed it. While at Gillette, they required marketing people to take a sales territory for six months, and mine was in Dallas, Texas, and up to Oklahoma. One of my best accounts was a small warehouse right on the state border. The buyer had a shotgun on the wall over his head and a spittoon next to his desk where he chewed tobacco and spit it out during my sales calls. Talk about Finding Your Purpose and using inspiration! I was determined to make my numbers. I didn't let him throw me, and we got along great. He ended up buying a ton of Right Guard from me. I figured if I could inspire him, I could motivate women to buy a lot of Mary Kay Cosmetics, and become members of my team. And I was right.

But here's the lesson. Even though I was using my Purpose of inspiring others, the job of recruiting women to sell cosmetics was just not for me. The lesson here is that you use your Purpose in endeavors that work for you. It's important that there are other aspects of your job, business, nonprofit, or wherever you invest your time mesh well with what you value, enjoy doing, or move you forward so that you can Hone Your Vision, Shift Your Energy, and Make Your Move. The three-step Strategic Process is a powerful prism to use as you utilize each of the 10 Pivot Points to keep you focused on where you would like to pivot next at any given stage of your life.

There I was, doing well in Mary Kay, but knowing that I needed to pivot to more fully mesh my Purpose and values. As a woman of faith, I was able to utilize another Pivot Point, and Have Patience, and wait for the right opportunity to surface. Granted, as a Type A person, I didn't just sit around and wait, I explored different ideas and dreams. Always a foodie and having a long-standing dream of owning my own restaurant someday, I used the time to research starting a soul food restaurant in Minneapolis called "Porches." There wasn't a good upscale soul food place in town, so I delved into that prospect as I also awaited the birth of my second child.

As it turned out, my Gillette mentor, Linda Keene, had also relocated to Minneapolis as a VP for the Pillsbury Company, in the Baked Goods Division. She called and let me know they were looking for a Director of Multicultural Marketing to help grow their business, given the 1990 Census was charting dramatic growth in consumers of color. Now, that touched directly into my value stream: inspiring others, especially corporations, to recognize, respect, and relevantly approach consumers of color. Honing my vision, shifting my energy, and making my move, I pivoted; I interviewed and got the job. The position made more sense for my growing family than starting a restaurant, but it was still in the food business and would consistently honor my Purpose.

I had the new job, new title, new office—and no budget. I was told to make the case to the three division VPs as to why they should fund a multicultural initiative. When I met with each of them, two of the three were willing to listen. However, the VP with the largest product portfolio, Refrigerated Dough and the Hungry Jack Biscuit Brand, promptly and politely told me that he didn't need my help. "Our sales are strong, and we already have lots of Black customers," he said. I had some inspiring to do for sure.

It's a lesson I had learned many times over: when your gift isn't working directly, look for another way to apply it. I knew I had to have his support. So, I asked him, "Since you are doing so well, may I shadow you on a few field trips to learn from you and find out why?" Those trips gave us a chance to get to know one another and for me to share some important knowledge about growing his core audience further as we went to different sales regions. I worked with the AC Nielsen research teams to uncover sales data to show that sales were higher in areas of concentrated ethnic demographics. The data was there, but the VP's team hadn't looked deeply into what the scanners were capturing. Inspiring the subject matter experts to be part of the initiative was helping to build the case. Yet I needed additional allies in the quest for budget dollars.

The Pillsbury Kitchens were run by Sally Peters, a consummate food professional with a Scandinavian background who ran the famous annual Pillsbury Bake-Off Contests and tested all the recipes that used Pillsbury products. I met with Sally and explained that she needed to understand that ethnic consumers may buy Pillsbury products, but would use them differently based on their culture. I convinced Sally to take a trip with me to key cities with

African American populations and great soul food restaurants to taste cultural dishes. As we talked, we came up with a plan for her team to also select five families in key Latino cities, send them boxes of Pillsbury products to fix meals the way they liked, and we would come for dinner. From these "experiments" Sally was inspired to see how Pillsbury products were used in totally different ways. Her teams took notes, and the participants shared many recipes.

Next, we still had to convince Pillsbury management, as well as our new UK management from the Grand Metropolitan company that had acquired Pillsbury in 1988, to support the multicultural initiative. I suggested to Sally that we develop a tasting seminar for the division called "Savor the Cultural Flavor," with samples prepared from the recipes we had collected through our travels. In addition, we would bring in key speakers from the restaurants, communities, and culinary experts to educate the Pillsbury/Grand Met brand teams and executives. The seminar was a *huge* hit. At the next quarterly planning session, the multicultural initiative received a budget of $5 million to get started, and the biggest part of the budget came from the VP of Refrigerated Dough. From 1990 to 1992, we created the first Spanish-speaking Pillsbury Doughboy commercials and targeted African American ads for the company. Pillsbury became active in events in cultural communities, and I even had the opportunity to meet the president of Mexico when he visited Los Angeles. At the other end of the spectrum, I was able to use my Purpose in the community of Minneapolis with a volunteer program Pillsbury sponsored called KAPOW—**K**ids **A**nd the **P**ower **O**f **W**ork. This was a mentorship program through which underserved youths of color from grade school to high school met executives of color who could show and tell them about career opportunities they otherwise might not have the chance to see up close. If they could see it, they could be it. It was another way to serve others that presented itself.

Finding Your Purpose and using it can be energizing across more than one platform as you Pivot for Success. Stay flexible and creative. Keep an open mind about what your purpose can do!

The Power of Purpose

It's my hope that you can see how Finding Your Purpose is a life-enhancing process. It can evolve over time, but your Purpose is always uniquely yours. Your Purpose may seem silly to people close to you, or it may feel like a long, hard dream to fulfill. But this Pivot Point is essential for success. It is your North Star and compass. As the late and legendary founder of Zappos, Tony Hseih, said, "When you walk with purpose, you collide with destiny." Purpose can drive you, corporations, governments, families, communities, teams, and more. The momentum that purpose can provide is what is so powerful. Purpose can align people and move mountains.

If you are struggling to define your Purpose, or defining it for the first time, here are some suggestions to try:

- Find some photos of yourself from key points in your life and spread them out. Take snapshots of them with your phone and put them on your computer so you can blow them up and look into your eyes. Find a time where your eyes are sparkling, and you seem excited about life. What were you doing then? Take note.
- List five things that you really enjoy doing, that you'd do for free if you could, and which would help others. This could be something from your present job or not.
- List five things that you don't enjoy doing, or which would benefit from improvements that you see are needed, but that could help others. Again, it could be in your current endeavors or not.

- Your purpose is trying to shine through. And if you are a late bloomer, rejoice! It's never too late to Find Your Purpose and thrive. As Steve Jobs said, "If you haven't found it yet, keep looking. Don't settle. As with all matters of the heart, you'll know when you find it."
- Your purpose needs to be flexible enough to embrace the changing flow of life as it evolves. Understand that the reed that bends is the reed that survives the storm.

2

Believing in Possibilities

When you've exhausted all possibilities remember this: You haven't.
—Thomas Edison

IN CHALLENGING TIMES like the 2020 pandemic, it may be hard to Believe in Possibilities. But believe we must. It is in the darkest of times when it's critical for us to turn our thoughts to what is possible to unleash the sparks of innovation that can create unseen opportunities and "out of the box" solutions to existing problems. Let's break down this Pivot Point.

To Believe is to accept something as true and to feel sure of that truth; to have faith in the truth or existence of something yet unseen; or to believe something or someone is capable of a particular action. Possibilities are a chance that something might exist, happen, or be true—and can be chosen from among a series of choices. What the dictionaries don't tell us is that what is most important is to not put a ceiling on possibilities. Just because something hasn't been done before does not mean it isn't possible. Whenever I get stuck with that thought, I think about Steve Jobs and Apple, and all the innovations he gave the world that we didn't even know we needed or wanted. Steve Jobs never got hung up with what was possible.

I also factor time and goals into Believing in Possibilities. What's your goal or dream? What's possible now to move toward your dream? What's possible a year from now? Five years from now? What resources do you have to make things happen? Who can help you? And how strong is your faith—your belief in yourself and the goal of your dream. You have to Believe in Possibilities when no one else does. When you break down both Believing and Possibilities with a focus on what your goals/dreams are within a workable time frame, you can more effectively pivot to Hone Your Vision, Shift Your Energy, and Make Your Move.

As a leader in business, your community, government, or your family, you will find that Believing in Possibilities affects not only you, but those around you. This Pivot Point is a renewable power source to energize and mobilize others when they may need it the most, particularly when they may not see the need, or don't see the vision. Show them the Possibilities.

Given the evolving ways we are living in a "new normal," many are considering staking out new paths of entrepreneurship, starting up side hustles, or thinking about changing jobs. To do so, it is critical to Believe in Possibilities that may not be readily evident. Understand you are not alone. The *Wall Street Journal* reported in September 2020 that Americans are starting businesses at the "fastest rate in more than a decade."[1] There were 3.2 million Employer Identification Number applications (tax IDs for new businesses) filed in 2020 versus 2.7 million at the same time in 2019. Imperative needs can emerge during a crisis and innovative solutions for

---

[1]Gwynn Guilford and Charity L. Scott, "Is It Insane to Start a Business During Coronavirus? Millions of Americans Don't Think So," *Wall Street Journal* (Sept. 26, 2020), p. 1, https://www.wsj.com/articles/is-it-insane-to-start-a-business-during-coronavirus-millions-of-americans-dont-think-so-11601092841?st=ssdvp6j134prp ji&reflink=article_copyURL_share&fbclid=IwAR29acRvrf2dZW9HWqCNL Asx_qe9UrNdZb3w9QBHtAbh_sjW0tPloyuJh68

them can create new business models. Trust me, starting a new business isn't easy, and many don't survive. Those that do have owners that keep Believing in Possibilities through thick and thin. I did, and I'll share more shortly on how I did it and how you can too.

Possibilities Abound for Those with Entrepreneurial Mindsets

But what if entrepreneurship isn't for you? As you have taken some time to Find Your Purpose, you may realize it may not be working for you. That's okay. Innovation is needed by every organization and industry large and small. There's a term that speaks to those who work within organizations and apply entrepreneurial thinking successfully—it's called Intrapreneurship. Proactive, action-oriented people with leadership skills who like to think outside the box will always be valued within organizations. That was me for many years until I made the leap into full-time entrepreneurship—twice.

In a 2018 article titled "Intrapreneurship Explained," the MIT Sloan School of Management cites some great examples of intrapreneurship that are right under our noses—Post-it Notes from 3M and Gmail from Google.[2] Those innovations did not start off as big strategic projects of either organization. Post-it Notes came about by accident and Gmail came from the 20% of company time given to employees to think "outside the box." Bill Aulet, the managing director of the Martin Trust Center for MIT Entrepreneurship, believes "Entrepreneurship is a way of creating value with new products, new ways of running businesses and with a number of assets you can control. But also, assets that you don't control. So, entrepreneurs can exist in corporations and corporations need

---

[2]Meredith Somers, "Intrapreneurship, Explained," MIT Sloan website—Ideas Made to Matter (June 21, 2018 edition), https://mitsloan.mit.edu/ideas-made-to-matter/intrapreneurship-explained

them more and more."[3] Organizations need people who can pivot from their current job description into something more because they Believe in Possibilities others can't see.

I cut my entrepreneurial teeth in corporate America. I intentionally worked for blue chip companies where I could learn from the best as I looked to a future of being my own boss. In every job I've had, I sought to do something that had not been done before that created value. Let me give you a quick time line:

Bloomingdale's—1978: Worked on the first television commercials for the company.

Gillette—1981–1991: Relaunched White Rain Shampoo; moved the Personal Care Division to target the Black consumer market; was on the team that acquired the first Black hair care company for a Fortune 500 corporation; worked at that acquisition and created more new products.

Pillsbury—1991–1992: Created the Multicultural Marketing department; within six months gained a $5 million budget for targeted advertising and programming.

Burrell Communications—1992–1994: Hired to merge three divisions, Advertising, Promotions, and Public Relations, into one company, Burrell Communications. As head of new business, sold consulting services and generated a new revenue stream that broke a 25-year record for new business.

L'Oréal/Soft Sheen Products—1999–2000: With my team and the sales team, launched two product lines that did $5 million each their first year; led the reformulation of over 100 products to L'Oréal standards as production moved from the family-owned plant to a modern L'Oréal facility; part of the team that acquired an $85 million Black hair care company to add to L'Oréal's portfolio.

---

[3]Somers, "Intrapreneurship, Explained."

Fashion Fair Cosmetics—2014–2016: As president, restruc-
tured the sales and marketing departments, revitalized the
e-commerce distribution channel, and contemporized the
advertising imagery and promotions for the business while
launching new products.

In all of these positions, I had to use the pivot of Believing in
Possibilities to inspire others to believe as well. Intrapreneurship
can be as challenging in as many ways as entrepreneurship. While
you are utilizing the company's resources and people, it can be hard
to change entrenched ways of doing things. I had to go through
many meetings and presentations, deal with naysayers, and endure
lots of "no's" internally and externally. With the foundation of
Believing in Possibilities and several of the other Pivot Points, such
as Getting Prepared, Seeking Positivity, Maintaining Persistence,
and Managing Perceptions, I was able to test my entrepreneurial
muscles within several corporate environments. It was a great way
to see if full entrepreneurship was right for me. If you have an entrepreneurial mindset, getting a regular paycheck while you satisfy that
yearning may be the way to go for you, too.

The L'Oréal/Soft Sheen story is an intriguing one of intrapreneurship with lots of lessons in Believing in Possibilities. First, a bit
of history.

Soft Sheen Products was a $100 million iconic Black-owned
hair care company out of Chicago, and the largest in the country.
They set the standard for all other Black hair care companies. Their
products were excellent, their distribution channels were strong in
both the retail and the professional salon markets, and their trade
show presentations were nothing short of amazing. The fashions,
hairstyles, and models they used drew huge crowds at the key annual
International Beauty Shows in New York City, Chicago, and the
Bronner Brothers historic Black-owned trade shows in Atlanta. At
these trade shows, while I worked for Gillette in the mid-1980s, I
saw the potential for the Black hair care market segment. And as a

fashionista from my Bloomingdale's days, I knew I wanted to be a part of it somehow.

Revlon had already jumped into the market with a relaxer for Black women called Realistic, which was gaining market share from Soft Sheen's Optimum relaxer. The "Relaxer Wars" had begun. According to people involved in the business during that time, Revlon began circulating rumors that Optimum's relaxer had ingredients in it that were damaging to the hair, to thwart Soft Sheen's sales. Ed Gardner, the founder and CEO of Soft Sheen, was a tall, elegant man who had won major respect from the Black community for his family's business success and philanthropy. I will never forget seeing him speak at the Soft Sheen booth at the New York Beauty Show about 1985. He said, "Revlon is trying to put us out of business with these lies about our products. We have *never* and will *never* put anything damaging to you into Soft Sheen's products. **We know your hair**. You have my word." I thought, "Wow! What a warrior. What an entrepreneur." He made me so proud that day.

About 10 years later, after the Gardner family made the decision to sell to L'Oréal, I was recruited to be the SVP of Marketing. Mr. Gardner's words were always in my mind as we developed new products. The multibillion-dollar global L'Oréal corporation had enormous technological capabilities in hair care that they wanted to bring to Soft Sheen. The R&D team traveled from Paris to Chicago to show us the newest advances in hair care that we should embrace. As head of marketing, I saw exciting intrapreneurial opportunities, for sure. But I also knew that L'Oréal did not know Black hair the way that the Soft Sheen team did. It was my job to fight for both the innovative technological advances that L'Oréal brought to the table, while also applying them to Black hair as Soft Sheen's R&D team indicated.

We had quarterly meetings with the executive management from L'Oréal Paris and Soft Sheen in New York, with us on one side of the table and them on the other. Prior to one meeting, the head of L'Oréal Paris R&D and I had the most intense discussion about why Black women did not want "squeaky clean hair" after shampooing like white women. We wanted hair that felt conditioned *and* clean, and then we'd condition it some more! He could not understand it. I needed to make sure he got my point at the next meeting where the global CEO of L'Oréal would be present. When you need to inspire others to Believe in Possibilities so they can pivot, there are times you must come prepared to make your case.

I came to the next meeting and set up a table with two dozen top-selling Black hair care shampoos so that the L'Oréal's Paris R&D head could examine the ingredients in them for himself. He looked them over with his lieutenants and they huddled together speaking in French. Finally, he said, "Aimee, I can see that this market is different. We will find a way to add our innovative technology to your market's expectations. But you must find a way to make your products comply with our manufacturing standards." We had a deal, and with L'Oréal's help, Soft Sheen developed an innovative line of anti-breakage shampoos, conditioners, and styling products.

Soft Sheen also needed to get into the hair color category more substantively, and who better than L'Oréal to help do that. Again, L'Oréal brought their technology. And Soft Sheen brought Black women's need for extra conditioning from their expertise in the professional salon business. The successful new color line was the first hair color kit for Black women with triple conditioning—before, during, and after coloring. And this time, L'Oréal Believed in Possibilities because several years later, their largest hair color line, Excellence, now has triple conditioning in its kit, offering conditioning before, during, and after coloring. This is something that I'm proud to see when I look at those kits in stores today and know that I and the Soft Sheen team had something to do with bringing that innovation and benefit positioning to L'Oréal.

My years at Soft Sheen were something else! It was the second time I had worked for a legacy African American built company, Burrell Communications being the first. It was a tremendous honor to have played a part in making sure that Ed Gardner's dream for Soft Sheen that I first heard at the New York International Beauty Show would live on after the L'Oréal acquisition.

If That Possibility Keeps Knocking at You, Believe It

After launching those two product lines at Soft Sheen for L'Oréal that each did $5 million in first year sales, and helping L'Oréal acquire another Black hair care company, Carson Products, I had to take a step back and say to myself, "How many times will I build new products for someone else and not my own family?" Enough was enough. Did I Believe in the Possibility I could do it for myself? Could I make the leap back into full entrepreneurship one more time?

My first go at starting my own business full-time was in 1995. Starting The Hilliard Group was a different opportunity. Consulting was pretty much banking on me giving advice to my clients. The start-up costs were low. I had been given a great launch by Tom Burrell, who became my first client, and through my speaking and networking efforts, I built up a comfortable business. I took the L'Oréal job four years later because I was traveling a lot for The Hilliard Group, had gone through a divorce, and did not like being away from my children as much as I was. They were getting too close to the nanny for me, even though she was wonderful.

After my success at L'Oréal/Soft Sheen, I thought about my entrepreneurship opportunities on another level. I asked myself, what do I have that I can bring to market? What's possible? What do I believe in that I could have more control of? I was at a crossroads and needed to pivot. I was still traveling too much. In fact, in January 1999, my daughter, who was graduating from middle school in *June*, asked me to please put the date on my calendar so I wouldn't miss it. I obviously needed to Hone My Vision, Shift My Energy, and Make a Move. And that's exactly what I did.

What I had to move with that people loved was my pound cake. I started making pound cake in college, because it was my favorite dessert and I got tired of buying cakes that did not taste like the homemade ones I loved. My mom only made one kind of cake . . .

the 1-2-3-4 cake. It was a basic yellow cake; she changed the icing depending on whose birthday it was. I figured if she could perfect one kind of cake, I could too. And that's what I set out to do—through trial and error, taste and refinement.

I loved to cook and had been my family's chief cook all during high school. That was my job, cooking dinner every night. For years after being on my own I always had massive amounts of leftovers because I only knew how to make food for six people at a time! I became the queen of dinner parties to use up the food, and always served my pound cake for dessert. After I got married and had my kids, I made it for bake sales. I even wrote a business plan outline on a yellow pad in 1988 for what I called "The Butter Batch Company"—and filed it away.

In 1999, still riding on the successes with Soft Sheen, I told myself that if one more person tells me I should put my cake on the market, I'm going to do it. At a neighborhood block party during the summer, a neighbor tasted a piece, looked me in the eye, and said, "Girl. This cake is *too* good. You *must* sell it in stores somewhere so I can buy it when I want some more!" That really set my mind in motion.

That Thanksgiving, as CFO (Chief Food Officer) for our annual Family Reunion/Food Fest—more than 35 people from all over the country came together for a full week—everyone demanded I make pound cake before the turkey and all the sides. That "observational research" confirmed there was demand. Then, I did something on a whim the day after Thanksgiving Day. We were in Baltimore, and there were some wonderful antique stores that I wanted to visit. I saw beautiful antique pedestal cake stands in several shops and bought about six of them. The guy I was dating at the time carefully packed them up at the UPS store and shipped them to Chicago. Why? Because I Believed in the Possibility. I had a vision of those pedestal cake stands being on a shelf in the office of my pound cake company. And that's exactly where they wound up. I still have them.

A month later, I had Christmas dinner with my dear friends Ken Smikle and Renee Ferguson, who always hosted Christmas at their home. I always brought my pound cake for dessert. For the holidays, I usually add some liquor over the warm cake to make it even more special. This particular Christmas, I must have really been feeling the holiday spirit, because I poured a *lot* of spirits over that pound cake. We were all enjoying our cake with ice cream after the sumptuous meal, talking about our dreams for the upcoming year, and I told everyone I finally was going to start a pound cake business! They all said, "Great idea! Bravo!" Then, they all started asking me, "Girl . . . what did you put in this cake? It sure is *goood* . . . It sure is COMFORTABLE!! This is a COMFORTABLE CAKE!!"

Ding, Ding, Ding!!!! My marketing bell started ringing loud and clear. *"That's It!!"* I exclaimed to everyone. "That's the name of the company! COMFORTCAKE!!!" And that is truly how the company name came into being. I observed how that name made people feel, and knew it had an emotional connection, and that connection was powerful. Ken told me to go home that night and get the domain name. Remember, this was 1999. Folks weren't buying a lot of food over the Internet. AOL was still sending discs to users in the mail. I didn't really get it yet, but just said okay, and went home and spent $35 to register the name with Registry.com. Now GoDaddy does it for a lot less!

However, my marketing background served me well, because I did one other thing. I went to USPTO.gov and with my own credit card, started the trademark process for ComfortCake. I was astonished to find the word was available, and even though the business plan had not been written, I knew the value of trademarks, and grabbed it immediately. It cost me $350. I didn't care. Getting that trademark and domain name were two of the best marketing moves I have ever made. I Believed in Possibilities and pivoted toward my dream—toward the road sign that said "GO!" My energy was shifting. The lesson: when you Believe in Possibilities, do what you can every step of the way toward making your dream real.

There I was, Honing My Vision and Shifting My Energy toward ComfortCake. I was still working at Soft Sheen and doing very well. So well, in fact, that the president of the New York division had spoken to me about my future with the company and asked me to consider moving to New York if they moved the Soft Sheen division there. It would mean a big promotion for me. The Spring of 2000 was a whirlwind. I hired one of my former employees to start writing a business plan for me, and when it was done, started going to banks and investors trying to get funds to start The ComfortCake Company. I was still doing my job at Soft Sheen and taking care of my family and my large, vintage home.

As I said at the beginning of this chapter, Believing in Possibilities means that you have to believe in the existence of something yet unseen and see the possibility in something that can be chosen from among a series of choices. Yet, even with my background of corporate success, banks wouldn't loan me any money. They told me a pound cake company was a "cute idea." Well, I couldn't see the money, but I started to believe I could see the possibility of finding some if I sold my home.

By November 2000, the clock was ticking. L'Oréal wanted a decision from me about moving to New York. I was sitting on the porch swing of my Chicago home on a Sunday, wrenching over the decision as I had to meet with the L'Oréal New York division president the next day. I was crying and swinging. My neighbors asked if I was okay, and I told them I was. And then, for the first time, I heard God speak to me. He said very clearly, "Take my hand and do ComfortCake." I didn't believe it, so I went inside, sat on the steps. And I heard it again. "Take my hand and do ComfortCake." I talked to my children, who I needed to be on board. My 11-year-old son knew I loved that porch swing, so he said, "Mom, we can get you a swing for inside another house." My 14-year-old daughter said, "Mom, a house is not a home. A home is the place you live with the people that you love." With their blessing, I made my move. I met with the L'Oréal division president the next day—Monday—and resigned, leaving a six-figure salary and more on the table. I incorporated The ComfortCake Company on February 15, 2001.

By late spring 2001, I put the house on the market, and my realtor, who became my first personal ComfortCake customer, came through in just five days with the highest offer for a home in our neighborhood. Then, she was able to get an offer done for a condo for us in a building about which I had once said, "If I ever sold my home, I'd love to live in that building." One of the best things about this Pivot Point is the momentum that can start once you take those first steps. Once people see the benefits of Believing in Possibilities, creativity opens up and amazing things can happen.

However, don't expect magic. Even though I believed deeply, I almost didn't go through with the sale. Major obstacles kept cropping up with the sale of my home. During the home inspection a huge, antiquated gas tank was found buried deep in the back yard that required removal and the grounds required environmental testing. Then the basement flooded after a major rainstorm—almost two feet of water. The buyers could have backed out, and I could have, too. But I kept Believing in Possibilities.

With the down payment from the house sale, I got the ComfortCake logo done by the same graphic artist who did the logo and swish for the Intel Inside brand. I Believed in the Possibility that ComfortCake would look like a national brand right from the start and convinced the artist to work with me. She's still a friend today. Then I hired a graphic arts team to design boxes and other packaging elements so we could present samples. This was the same team that did the design for the NutraSweet brand. Again, I was willing to pay for people who understood my vision and could help others Believe in the Possibility of ComfortCake. They did a terrific job; we have never had to redesign any of our logos or major package elements.

Next, I needed to get a bakery to make samples. The Yellow Pages was still the "go to" back then—and that's what I used.

I cold-called commercial bakeries. Several of them said, "Sure, just come over and show me your recipe and I'll let you know if we can make it." Well, that wasn't going to happen. I had done my research and knew that showing my recipe without having a Non-Disclosure Agreement (NDA) signed first, meant that my recipe could be used without my permission. I spoke with more than 10 bakeries and insisted on each signing a NDA before moving forward. Those that wouldn't, I did not engage with. Finally, I spoke with a very large bakery that said they couldn't work with such a small project, but they owned a smaller family-run bakery that probably could, and to give them a call. I did, they signed the NDA, and created wonderful samples for me.

I needed those samples because I had been Believing in Possibilities for a while by then. As a corporate executive, I traveled a lot and had never had pound cake on my flights with meals. Socially, I had met and befriended Sandra Rand, the manager of Supplier Diversity of United Airlines. I had told her of my dream of starting The ComfortCake Company some time before and asked if she could help me get a meeting with the buyer at United when I was ready. I wanted to see what they might need and want. She said sure, just let her know when I was ready. Well, I was ready, and she set up the meeting.

I met with the buyer at United's purchasing headquarters. I brought my samples in a professional sample box, each individually wrapped just as United's customers would eat them on the plane. We talked about how he made purchase decisions, general pricing, and other parameters. He thanked me for coming and I left.

The very next day, I got a call from the buyer. He said, "Amy, we like your samples very much. We'd like to buy 550,000 slices for our next purchasing cycle." I was in shock. So much so that I said, "Thank you very much," and hung up the phone. A true story! I quickly recovered, though, called him right back, and we got the contract. United Airlines was our first customer.

That's Believing in Possibilities in action. And if it worked for me countless times, there is no reason you can't Believe in Possibilities, too.

P↑↓VOT

Believing Is Everything, but Be Specific

Making the pivot by Believing in Possibilities to start The Comfort-Cake Company as a 48-year-old single mom with two children to put through college was risky. But I have a high tolerance for risk. When you use this Pivot Point, **know yourself**. I knew I did not want to be 85 years old and regret not following this dream.

Let's review some of the other lessons of Believing in Possibilities:

- To successfully pivot toward your dream, new direction, adventure, or lifeline you not only need to Find Your Purpose, but it is essential to Believe in it. The mind is an incredible muscle that can be trained to think you can or you can't. And for me, having faith is paramount.
- Believing in Possibilities is more specific than "You can do it!" It requires you to look objectively at your dream or goal. What is possible to do about it now? A month from now? A year from now? Five years from now? Who can help you? What small steps can you take to start making it happen?
- Specifically, for businesspeople, if you want to be an entrepreneur, great. There are many books on how to start a business. If owning your own business is not what you want, there are options.

- Intrapreneurship is a totally viable way to distinguish yourself and create value in corporate America while testing your entrepreneurial muscles. In fact, it is becoming a critical skill needed by many organizations.
- Whatever your dream or goal is, remember that Believing in Possibilities is not magic. You must believe deeply enough in yourself, sustain that belief in yourself and others—enough to weather the inevitable naysayers, storms of doubt, and obstacles that will come your way in the process of making things happen.
- Always remember that Believing in Possibilities opens up incredible creativity and motivating momentum in others that allows amazing things to unfold.

3

Defining Your Priorities

For where your treasure is, there your heart will be also.

—*Matthew 6:21*

TODAY MORE THAN ever, Defining Your Priorities is a critical step before you can emotionally, energetically, and strategically pivot toward the vision you have for your life. Defining Your Priorities determines where you will put your time, your resources, and your mental fortitude every day. Your priorities are what come before everything else. Prioritizing, of course, and the degree of it, will depend on what part of your life you are focusing on—work, family, relationships, health, spirituality—and where you are in life, whether you are a student, single, married, parent, executive, entrepreneur, and so on. These two aspects—where you are in life and what part of your life you focus on—both have great impact on how you Define Your Priorities.

It's also important to understand the difference between a priority and a goal. As a business executive, a goal for your division could be to hit a 10% sales growth target over the prior year. Priorities would be to make sure that your sales team is making more calls per month, the sales materials are updated, and new products roll out on time.

With research, you'll find many templates that can be used to set your priorities. I encourage you to find one that feels right for you. Writing your priorities down—seeing them in black and white—is a reminder of what you want to achieve. For me, and for many others, it is vital to do this to avoid becoming burned out or overwhelmed by a "to do" list that is too long to complete in a reasonable amount of time.

When I Define My Priorities each year, I first look at the big picture of what I want to achieve. I ask myself some clarifying questions:

- If I had five years left to live, what would I do?
- If I then learn I only have three years left, what would fall off the list?
- If, God forbid, I found out I only had one year left, what would I want to do?
- Why aren't I doing that NOW?

This may seem overly simplistic, however; no one knows when their time is up. The COVID-19 pandemic has made this abundantly clear. Each day is a gift, and your energy is a finite resource. If you cannot pivot to Define Your Priorities based on the most important parts of your life, the result may be frustration, anxiety, and a feeling that you have to do it all. That does not set you up for success.

Priorities Can Shift

Understand that Defining Your Priorities can and will shift. And they should. They certainly will shift if you have children, for example. They will shift when your goals change. The questions I ask myself every year are a dramatic reminder to keep the main thing the main thing. If your goal is to become the CEO, then what Priorities do you need to define this year, right now, to reach that goal? You can certainly Define Your Priorities beyond right now or beyond this year. But at the end of the day, it's critical to stay focused on what is most important to accomplish in each of your top life buckets. By doing so, you will continue your forward momentum. And, you'll find you will feel more comfortable saying "no" to activities that are not priorities for you. You will be able to more quickly screen options and make better decisions about how you spend your time, resources, and energy. In a nutshell, Defining Your Priorities helps you with Honing of Your Vision with greater clarity.

A crisis can change your priorities immediately. For this reason, Defining Your Priorities must act as guideposts, but remain fluid, based on the situation at hand. Work situations, health issues, economic issues—all can change what gets done first. As you become more adept at being able to Define Your Priorities, you can pivot quickly when you need to, making sound decisions and guiding others who depend on your leadership to follow you as well. Here's an example:

As a relatively new product manager at Gillette in 1984, I was given a plum assignment to manage the Personal Care Division's annual Miss America Promotion. The Miss America Promotion was the division's largest consumer and trade promotion, involving all the major brands and retail customers, and brought in multimillions of dollars in sales and profits. Each year, the marketing and sales teams would eagerly watch the pageant to see which contestant would win, as she would be the spokesperson around whom the promotion would be built. All advertising, public relations, and in-store displays would carry Miss America's picture, and she would engage with key accounts and meet consumer contest winners. Well, imagine my profound surprise and joy when that year Vanessa Williams was crowned Miss America! The first Black Miss America ever. History was made. I was ecstatic. I began Defining

My Priorities immediately based on my goal: this Miss America Promotion had to be the most successful one Gillette had ever had.

And it certainly started out that way. Vanessa Williams was the most popular Miss America in a long time. Not only was she historic, but she was also gracious, personable, and all around lovely to work with. All the trade customers wanted her to visit their headquarters, and she was on countless television shows. She was so popular, it was hard for Gillette to get her for bookings. One of my efforts was to involve Black magazines. *Essence* magazine did a special promotional insert and contest featuring Vanessa Williams that was a tremendous hit. Sales were going through the roof.

Then the roof collapsed.

Early one Wednesday morning, the SVP of our ad agency called me and told me to go stand by the fax machine. I stood there in total shock as the nude photos of Vanessa Williams came through. These photos had been taken much earlier in her modeling career and were published without her authorization. The news broke over the airwaves, and within minutes the president of the division called an emergency meeting of all the top people involved with the promotion. It was crisis management time! As we awaited the decision of the Miss America organization about Ms. Williams's future, we had to pivot immediately to ensure the stability of our trade and consumer promotions. The following week 50,000 displays were scheduled to ship for one of our biggest accounts; it had a beautiful picture of Ms. Williams on it. I was so proud of that photo shoot.

The president of the division looked down the table directly at me and said, "Amy, you are Damage Control Central. We are not to lose one account over this. Fix all those displays immediately, and any other new ones due to go out." Talk about making a pivot and Defining Your Priorities. Whew!

I knew what I had to do. In crisis times like that, it is critical to stay cool and use laser focus to Define the Priorities for the team. As a leader, you cannot fold or get emotional—you have a job to do. People are looking to you for guidance and assurance that things will be okay. It is in these moments where pivoting is important. You'll recognize the need, as you have done many times. Like a well-oiled machine, you can switch it on immediately when and if you must.

That is exactly what I did. Gathering up the sales, ad agency, packaging, and graphic teams in a "War Room," we mapped out our options. Within an hour, we had a solution—shoot a photo of a crown, a dozen red roses, and a scepter representing a crowned Miss America using the same copy and display size of the planned promotions. We had the alternate shoot done the next day and switched out the placards in time for the displays to be shipped out on time. We did not miss a sale or lose a customer.

It was an incredible week of change and crisis management. At work, I had my "Fight Face" on. At home, I was devastated. What a loss, and I felt it personally. And yet, I learned extraordinary lessons in real time about pivoting. Keep your eye on your goal. Define Your Priorities and move forward. Hone Your Vision. Shift Your Energy and Make Your Move. I had to, and so did Vanessa Williams. I got promoted and my career at Gillette kept rising. Vanessa Williams rose from the ashes, recreated her career, and has done very well. She and I have kept in touch over the years, and I'm very proud of her.

Years later, I wanted to start my food company so I Defined My Priorities. As I mentioned in Believing in Possibilities (Pivot Point #2), I sold my home to start The ComfortCake Company. We got off to a huge start with the United Airlines order for 550,000 slices. I was ecstatic! But then we had to get it produced. I returned to the small bakery that made our delicious samples and told the owner about the order. He asked me to wait outside his office. I waited for almost 90 minutes. Clearly something was not right. I did not feel respected given the business I was bringing in. When I was finally called back in, he told me he'd *try* to get the order done. Well, that was not going to work for me. My Priorities were clearly Defined. I had a big important customer that was going to give credibility to my business. We had to deliver. I wrestled with the bakery for two months. It was clear to me that this bakery was not large enough to handle an order of that size, so I had to fire them. My decision was not only because of their size, but because of how I was treated as a customer. When your Priorities are clear, it is easier to make hard decisions. Now I had a big order and no bakery to make it. This was in late May 2001 and the order was due to be on board by September 15, 2001. However, we had to have production samples for United to taste by August.

A year earlier, I had been to a good friend's holiday party and met a well-known dessert entrepreneur, Marc Shulman of Eli's Cheese-cake in Chicago. We shared stories about the business; he thought my idea for ComfortCake was great and offered his help. He was so generous, giving advice and support for product testing and label-ing. Now, with mere months to fulfill the order for United Airlines and no facility to make the pound cake, I needed help—like yester-day! Pivoting back to Believing in Possibilities, I called Marc. He gave me the name of a large commercial bakery that specialized in the airline business and told me to use his name to get a meeting. I called right away, explained my dilemma, and got a meeting for the next day. We signed the NDA, I met the staff, and toured the bakery; it was just what I was looking for. I worked with the product developer to get my recipe right—United wanted a vanilla flavor, which was going to be new for ComfortCake—and they told me to come back to taste samples in two weeks, after they gathered all the raw materials for the process.

United Airlines wanted to taste production samples also. I prayed that I could use the new bakery samples for United. As it was, I knew we would be late for the first September shipment date United wanted. This is when I had to use Pivot Point #10—Manag-ing Perceptions, which I'll share more about later. In a nutshell, I had to be honest with my customer and ask for a shipment exten-sion delivery date. It would have done me no good to try and push to make a deadline that was not feasible. I certainly wasn't going to deliver an inferior cake. Because I was getting advice from such a well-known food entrepreneur, and United knew the bakery I was using, they gave me an extension to ship them by October 15, 2001.

When I walked in that August with my small team to taste the samples, I felt like Mrs. Fields! There were two long tables with samples laid out in precise rows. The tasting went well, the production samples were produced, and United approved them. We prepared and went into production for the October order.

Then came September 11, 2001. That's right. 9/11.

When the planes hit the Twin Towers in New York, the Pentagon in DC, and crashed in a field in Pennsylvania, the country was paralyzed. Airline travel almost ground to a halt. I thought our order would be cancelled. United Airlines, however, thought a product called ComfortCake would sound good to customers and kept us on board for the October 15 order, and expanded it for their international flights to South America. However, the bakery didn't fare as well because so much of their business was with the airline industry. Their cash flow took a substantial hit. I tried to call the bakery owner to talk about a new order and couldn't get him on the phone. Finally, on a Friday, he told me to call him the next Monday. When you Define Your Priorities, that means you make sure that things are being done that need to be done. You engage with more than one person on a team, getting to know others who are central to your success. I had gotten to know the product developer at the bakery well and had her home number. Not wanting to wait until Monday for information, I called her on Saturday and asked, "What's going on with the bakery?" She said, "Amy, I don't know, but we haven't been paid in two weeks."

I spoke to the owner on Monday and he was bereft. He told me very sadly that he had tried everything, but the bank was coming at noon on Tuesday to shut him down. When a bank shuts a company down, they seize all assets on the property. I had spent $45,000 on commercial Bundt cake pans to produce ComfortCake for our new website for Thanksgiving and they were at that bakery. We had

6,000 red boxes ready to be shipped there that week. Talk about Defining My Priorities! I gathered my team around our small conference table and told them the news. I said, "We have five minutes to have a pity party." Then, I told our operations manager to secure a U-Haul for first thing Tuesday morning. I told my assistant I'd pick her up at 7:00 a.m. because we needed to be at the bakery by 8:00.

We got there at 8:15 due to traffic. I was a bit frantic yet stayed cool with silent prayer. My operations manager was already there loading up our pans. I talked to the owner, thanked him for treating us so well, and told him how sorry I was about his business. I hugged the product development manager, who was in tears. Then, the bakery's purchasing manager quietly asked me to come into his office. "Amy," he said as he handed me some computer printouts, "these are your actual cost of goods. I know of a bakery not far from here that can produce for you. With these numbers you'll know that you are getting the right profits." Wow. What an incredible gesture.

Maintaining my vision for ComfortCake, we were able to Shift our Energy and Make our Move. By keeping my Priorities Defined, and Believing in Possibilities, we left the bakery with the equipment we needed to keep the business going and the critical information to keep it profitable while onboarding a new bakery. It shows as well how the different Pivot Points interact and intersect with each other. The experience with having to change bakeries—twice—did not require me to just Define and Redefine My Priorities. It also required me to employ Getting Prepared (#5), use Having Patience (#6), continue Seeking Positivity (#7), and Maintain Perseverance (#9) during this time.

Opportunities Shift Priorities Also

Defining Your Priorities is not only critical during crises, but this important Pivot Point also helps you identify opportunities. I often use Gary Keller's book *The One Thing* when Defining My Priorities. He suggests you identify the *one thing* that will make all aspects of your life better within a given point in time. With that done, you can then focus on and prioritize the other aspects of your life that will allow you to accomplish that *one thing*. This will also make your life better in the process. As you can tell, I believe Defining Your Priorities is not something you can just do in your head and be done. This needs to be written down. This needs to be specific. This is your life.

I'm a big fan of journaling, just like the Queen of England is. Every evening she writes in her journal. While I don't write every night, I have journals that go back 45 years. They chart my evolving life goals and priorities. Journaling helps clear my head and download the mental clutter so I can focus on Defining My Priorities as I move forward. I'm not perfect, but I do like making progress, as my friend and mentor Sheryl Sandberg often advises.

On a personal front, working well with people at all levels has always been a Defining Priority for me. Growing up, I saw my parents do this. They were both involved in the community, gave back of their time and talents, and could talk to anyone, from governors to grocery clerks, and treated them all the same. I've been told I have those same traits; at least I strive to do so. It has served me well in entrepreneurial and corporate environments. Often, the people who hold the keys of access to decision makers can themselves be decision makers. People are people, respect always is appreciated, and no one has a lock on good ideas.

One of my Priorities when I was in high school was to go to Howard University. Several family members had attended, and it was a hallmark of Black achievement. The only way I could go to Howard was if I got a scholarship, because I had a full scholarship to Michigan State. Believing in Possibilities, working with my high school speech teacher, I attended Howard University on a Debate Team Scholarship. I was involved in student government, pledged Delta Sigma Theta sorority, and worked part-time as a sales clerk in fashion boutiques in Georgetown. I majored in home economics, so I could take fashion merchandising, and minored in business.

I wanted to become a fashion buyer and have my own store one day. I Defined My Priorities while at Howard to keep my scholarship, be involved in campus life, have fun, meet lots of people, make my own money, and graduate on time. Doing those things allowed me to have some extraordinary experiences. It was purposeful to work alongside my Howard classmate Elijah Cummings on the Liberal Arts Student Council, and then to see him rise to become one of the foremost congressional representatives in America. We remained friends until his untimely passing.

What fun it was to be on the Homecoming Committee and create the first Howard Homecoming Fashion Show, which became an annual event for decades. Because one of my Priorities was to be one of the best sales clerks at the boutique where I worked in Georgetown, a Polaroid sales manager noticed my work ethic when he was shopping there with his wife. I was invited to lead a team and travel the southeastern United States training Polaroid distributors on the innovative SX-70 Camera—when I was only 19 years old. I was able to participate in the national product launch of the camera at the Fontainebleau Hotel in Miami, complete with huge SX-70 letters in carved ice and spotlights shining through. I met Edwin Land, the inventor of the Polaroid camera. My eyes were opened to how big business did things.

My Priority to be so involved in everything I could at Howard saved my sanity the fall of my junior year when my best friend was brutally murdered by her fiancé. It was a horrible time, and still haunts me. Yet because I knew that graduating on time was my goal, keeping myself busy became the key Priority I leaned on to Pivot my mind and Shift My Energy so I could keep moving through my grief.

Hold on to Your Core Values as Priorities Evolve

I hope you can see how Defining Your Priorities evolves as your life evolves. However, as your life changes, your core values do not have to. Respecting others, family, faith, building a business, staying healthy, maintaining good relationships—these core values have always been at my center. You have to define what your core values are.

Here's one way of explaining it. Think of the amoeba. I didn't like chemistry or biology in college but had to take the courses to graduate. In them I learned about amoebas. Amoebas have a core cell, but their boundaries stretch and grow to embrace their changing surroundings. That's how I think of the Defining Your Priorities. You hold on to your core values as you work toward and honor what you would do if you knew you only had a year left to live. The visual of an amoeba came to me as I thought about how your life changes, as that year extends to two, five, ten years, and beyond and you recalibrate your priorities. You can Define and Redefine Your Priorities to align with the changes in your life situation, but your core values can remain steadfast.

Building authentic relationships has been a core Defining Priority for me, and I've been blessed to have built some great ones. While at Howard, I spent each Thanksgiving at the home of a family friend from Detroit, Darwin Davis, who lived in Stamford, Connecticut. He was the first African American to make the Million Dollar Round Table in Sales for the Equitable Life Insurance Company. This man pivoted from selling my dad insurance at our kitchen table part-time when he was still a teacher to becoming a millionaire. At his home on those Thanksgivings, I met Earl Graves Sr., the publisher of *Black Enterprise* magazine; Frank Mingo, the first Black VP in Account Management at the J. Walter Thompson ad agency; and Carolyn Jones, the first Black VP of Creative at the BBDO ad agency and the writer of the iconic "We Do Chicken Right" slogan for Kentucky Fried Chicken. All three became mentors to me after I began my marketing career while at Harvard Business School and beyond. Frank Mingo and Carolyn Jones were role models as I worked in advertising. Earl Graves recommended me for the Howard University Board of Trustees and the PepsiCo Multicultural Advisory Board and became a dear friend. I worked hard to give back to those relationships. I wanted them to be proud of me and to represent them well.

A key shift in Defining My Priorities revolved around the choices I made when I married and had children. As a woman, I do believe you can have it all if you want, just not at the same time, and not without a price. I am an ambitious person and always have been. With a family, however, it could not be just about me. We almost lost my daughter at birth when she became tangled in her umbilical cord and I needed an emergency caesarean section. I wrote about this challenging time in a story called "Mother Wit" for *Chicken Soup for the Mother's Soul,* which was published by Jack Canfield and Mark Victor Hanson. From that experience my Priorities were Defined that I would never put my ambitions before my children. I would find a way to make sure they knew I was there for them always. My husband and I were not as successful at Defining our Priorities with each other, and our divorce was hard. It was a Defined Priority for us, though, to maintain a wonderful relationship with our children together; that has been a true joy as they remain close to us both.

When it comes to my career and my businesses, however, I could have gone even harder for the brass rings of corporate life. I could have structured my businesses—both consulting/speaking and ComfortCake—to be much larger. But I knew myself. That was not what I wanted. That may have worked for others, and I'm sure it has, and it may work for you. But for me, I wanted the flexibility to be at school plays and T-ball games, to host sleepovers, and have regular Blockbuster movie nights. Those were Defined Priorities—my time with my kids.

I also made sure my children were involved with the Comfort-Cake business, too, from Day 1. At 14, my daughter, Angelica, wrote our trademarked slogan, "Pound Cake So Good It Feels Like a Hug." I have been able to gain major business from just saying that slogan. I cold called 7-Eleven headquarters and the EVP of Merchandising just happened to answer the phone while her assistant was at lunch. I told her who I was and what we made. She loved the slogan so much we got a meeting and sold ComfortCake to 2,100 stores! My daughter now has a great career going in advertising.

At age 11, my son, Nick, was a chief taste tester when I brought samples home; he came up with the solution for our Chocolate Chip–flavor pound cake when the bakery couldn't get it right. "There's too much flour in it, Mom," he said. He was correct, and the bakery team was floored! When Nick asked me about the business one evening when he was in high school, I handed him the Profit and Loss statements to study and told him, "That's ComfortCake right here." We studied them together. He was a finance major in college, graduated Magna Cum Laude, and is now enjoying a consulting career.

When considering the entrepreneurial path, it is often recommended that you decide if you want a lifestyle business or a high-growth business. I chose a lifestyle business with intellectual property that I could license and monetize down the road. I Defined My Priorities to meet the goals of flexibility and creating enough substantive financial wealth for my family to pay back my investors and make the sacrifices worthwhile. This is a work in progress. I would not trade my entrepreneurial flexibility for anything.

When my dad became very ill in 2007, I needed to be in Detroit for long stretches to assist my mom with his care. The recession hit in 2008, but ComfortCake's biggest customer, the Chicago Public Schools, kept us afloat. By 2009, we were selling CPS six million servings a year. But I do not regret at all being there for my mom during those hard years before my dad passed in February 2009, right after Barack Obama's inauguration the previous month. Both of my parents could not believe they were able to see a Black man elected president. My dad couldn't speak by that time, but I asked him if we could take Mom to the inauguration, as she didn't want to leave his side. He squeezed my hand, yes. Being in Washington

DC to witness history on that freezing cold day was something my mom truly treasured. And I didn't have to ask anyone for permission to be there.

P↕VOT

Always Define Your Priorities for Yourself

As social media makes it seem like everyone else is living the high life, make sure you are living the life that works for *you*, and living what's important to *you*. Going for the shine can be tempting, but the shine can tarnish before you know it. Often, what's behind the curtain is like what was revealed in the *Wizard of Oz* . . . a facade. For example, I've had plenty of opportunities to make lots of money by cutting deals "under the table." But I always declined because integrity was a high priority for me. I had to sleep at night.

If you are stuck in a bind about what's really important to you, try these steps:

- Identify what major life buckets are central to your life right now: work, family, relationships, health, spirituality, etc.
- Chart where are you in life right now: single, married, parent, executive, entrepreneur, artist, etc.
- What are your key values? Be deeply honest. It does no good to put down what others think you "should" value.
- Answer the Clarifying Questions about what you would do if you knew you had five, three, or one year left to live and what would fall off the list with each diminishing time period. What would your priorities be?

- Then, in reverse, configure the Clarifying Questions for the next one, three, and five years from now, assuming you are going to be here. How will your priorities change?
- Keep your core values, where you are in life, and what parts of your life are central in mind as you go through this exercise. You'll be surprised at the clarity this will bring to Defining Your Priorities and will make this pivot easier.

4

Envisioning Prosperity

Making a living is not the same as making a life, because all money isn't green.

WE HAVE ALL heard stories of very wealthy people who, on their deathbeds, wished they had spent more time with their family and friends instead of building their empires. Don't get me wrong. You need money in life. And not just for basic food, clothing, and shelter. To make a sustaining mark, to build a company, to assist others in a substantive way or leave a legacy, to build generational wealth, you need to have money or obtain it. It's what you do with money that can determine your satisfaction in life, based on your values, Defined Priorities, and what makes you feel prosperous.

Most definitions of prosperity involve economics and lots of wealth. I prefer to think of prosperity as living a rich and full life with all the money and happiness you need. Why? Because how much is up to the individual—prosperity is not one size fits all. In my speeches, I often ask people, "Do you know how much your enough is?" Most look back at me blankly and shake their heads. If you haven't been tested as to how much you can really live on and be happy, you might not know. One of my good friends sent me a great saying: "One of the best things in life is realizing you're perfectly happy without the things you thought you needed the most." I couldn't agree more.

But I didn't always think so.

Like most Type A people, I spent years relentlessly going for the gold—the brass ring. There is nothing wrong with that. I admire those who are able to do so, have good relationships with family and friends, stay grounded, have balanced values, and being, quite frankly, rich. Again, though, I know myself and have learned what I can and can't do, will and won't do, depending on the other Priorities in my life.

There are times in life when your hustle has to be hard. When I was just out of college and grad school, I had my hustle on for sure. Building my businesses took tremendous commitment, as did raising my family. I'm still going for the gold, but I've realized over the years that I want to glide more and grind less. With focus, and knowing what I really need, I'm much more able to pivot toward Envisioning Prosperity as it works for me. That's the beauty of these 10 Pivot Points. They are flexible. They can be used to fit your life and your life stages and will keep you focused during the process.

When I got my first job out of college, in the Designer department of Bloomingdale's, I thought nothing about spending almost a month's rent on a pair of gray Valentino Couture pants. I was single, and when I wore them with a sleek black turtleneck, silver jewelry, good shoes, and a great bag, I looked like a million bucks, especially when I went to fashion shows. Making my way up the corporate ladder, I had to look the part, so spending my hard-earned money on a good work wardrobe was an investment in my eyes. My mom taught me how to shop well for quality on sale, and I took her lessons to heart. Looking the part was key for others to perceive you as leadership material. And that required money.

Dressing for the job you want rather than the job you have is still important, but perhaps not as common as it once was—and the

COVID-19 pandemic and Zoom meetings have changed that significantly. Today, staying current with technology is nonnegotiable and not cheap. To Envision Prosperity in just about any platform, you must be able to connect with others, so being able to afford to do so is critical.

Know What Your Enough Is

As a Boomer, my peers and I were taught if we went to college, and got a job, we'd be on our way to a prosperous life. Today, the route to prosperity is changing. There is a major debate going on about the value of college degrees and MBAs. In a recent *Wall Street Journal* article, Elon Musk of Tesla criticized the "MBA-tization of America business," saying it has hampered innovation.[1] Where an MBA degree used to be a guarantee of a prosperous economic future, today's recent college graduates can't find jobs and are returning home to live with their parents until they find employment. All with heavy student loan debt to pay. MBA degrees at top schools can cost six figures per year. Generations X, Y, and Millennials are struggling to see a future with their own homes to raise their families. The prosperity picture, when measured in mere dollars, can look pretty bleak. However, what matters is your perspective, and how you Hone Your Vision, Shift Your Energy, and Make Your Move.

Years ago, a dear friend was grinding hard to work her way up the ladder in media sales. She was a beast, incredibly driven. She was also a warm and gracious woman, loved by many. When she received a huge promotion that came with a significant bump in salary, everyone was thrilled for her. I will never forget, however, seeing her become thin and looking very stressed from the pressures of the job. One day after church, I congratulated her on her success, as I heard she was breaking records. To my surprise, she looked me

---

[1]Patrick Thomas, "Elon Musk Decries M.B.A.-zation of America" *Wall Street Journal* (December 9, 2020), https://www.wsj.com/articles/elon-musk-decries-m-b-a-ization-of-america-11607548589?mod=searchresults_pos5&page=1

in the eye as if to warn me and said, "Amy, never forget. All money isn't green." Not long after that, she passed away suddenly at the prime of her life.

I have seen stress take a toll on too many people close to me. In the 18 months *before* the COVID pandemic, I lost *nine* close friends, mentors, and mentees who were hard-working executives, entrepreneurs, and educators—all of whom passed away from cancers or heart disease. One right after the other. All too soon. All were under great professional stress. The pressure of "making it" in America, particularly as a person of color, is intense, no matter how many degrees you have. Systemic racism is real. So is gender discrimination. Yet so is the American Dream. Going for it and wanting the traditional definition of prosperity is something everyone should have the chance to achieve. But I am here to tell you, it can take a toll, and it is imperative to guard against that toll.

As the September 2020 Women in the Workplace report by McKinsey and LeanIn.org cited, women are leaving corporate America faster than ever before.[2] After all the strides made to move women forward, not enough has been done to recognize what is needed to work at the intense pace required from corporations and successfully maintain a more balanced life. African American women are among the most well-educated and are starting businesses at a rate faster than any other demographic group. Yet obtaining capital to finance businesses is still as difficult as it was when I started The ComfortCake Company almost 20 years ago. According to *Fast Company* magazine, less than 3% of venture capital goes to women-owned businesses, and less than 0.2% goes to female founders of color.[3] Instead, what women are doing is to pivot

[2]Sarah Coury, Jess Huang, Ankur Kumar, Sara Prince, Alexis Krivkovich, and Lareina Yee, "Women in the Workplace 2020," McKinsey & Co. website (Sept. 30, 2020), https://www.mckinsey.com/featured-insights/diversity-and-inclusion/women-in-the-workplace

[3]Kathryn Ross and Katica Roy, "How Corporate Venture Capital Could Close the Gender Gap for Entrepreneurs," Fast Company (Sept. 9, 2020), https://www.fast-company.com/90548188/how-corporate-venture-capital-could-close-the-gender-gap-for-entrepreneurs

toward Envisioning Prosperity on their own terms. And they are not alone.

My son, who is in his early thirties, has friends who live at home with their parents to save money to buy their own homes or businesses. They do this because they made the Pivot to Envisioning Prosperity and realized it's necessary to achieve their Priorities. This is, actually, a time-honored way of living: multigenerational living under one roof. Many cultures have done this for generations, but it is viewed as a new, if not regressive, phenomenon by a lot of Americans. It isn't that way for many who have immigrated to our shores. Often, people wonder how certain cultures can own multiple 7-Eleven franchise stores, cleaners, restaurants, or other small businesses after coming here with very limited funds. As a multicultural marketer, I have studied entrepreneurship across the many cultures that live in America, and a consistent theme that is shared is multigenerational living and pooled resources to Envision Prosperity as a family. So, what we are experiencing now with college graduates moving home after college can be viewed not as a burden, but as a time-tested way to build wealth. It is all in how you look at it.

My daughter moved back home after two years of college. I raised my children to know that by the time they turned 18 years old, they would be on their way to college or have a job. But they would not be living with me; I wanted to foster a sense of independence in them. I admit, I pushed my daughter hard to go to college right after high school even though in my heart I felt a gap year would have been a good move for her. We lived in the big city of Chicago, and Angelica went to Hampton University, a Historically Black College in Hampton, Virginia, a small city near the coast. While she enjoyed her time there, she called and told me, "Mom, I'm having 'skyscraper withdrawal' and I want to come home to work." The lesson for me? My "traditional" path to Envisioning Prosperity did not fit her path. This was a pivotal realization for me! When I was young, I couldn't wait to go straight to college and graduate right on time and keep moving toward my career. Change plans? Take a break from college? No way. As a mother, however, I had to step back and allow my child to carve her own path. Angelica liked to work. She still does.

We had to strike an agreement, though. I said, "You can come home, but you will need to find a job within six months. And if you cannot find an apartment within that time, we'll need to work out a rent agreement." Whew. That felt and sounded a bit harsh even to me as I said it—tough love. My goal was to continue to foster Angelica's independence and let her know I believed in the strong work ethic Angelica had shown when she helped out at The ComfortCake Company during summers.

Angelica stepped up to the plate and met those benchmarks. On her own, she found a great job as a marketing intern at a nationally renowned research company that annually compiled the spending patterns of African Americans and whose data was used by the *Wall Street Journal*, *Ad Age*, *New York Times*, Nielsen, and many other resources consulted by corporate America. That was a Proud Mama moment. Another was when she announced she found an apartment within our agreed time frame. After working for the market research company, Angelica came to work for The ComfortCake Company full-time. She also went to college at night, earning her degree in marketing from the University of Phoenix. Little did I know how much Angelica's incredible work ethic would become pivotal to Envisioning Prosperity for me and The ComfortCake Company down the road.

For many of the 10 Pivot Points, you'll hear me repeat "Know Thyself." Know, or at least take the time to step back and assess how you feel in your gut about the opportunities, forks in the road, adventures, lifelines, career moves, relationships, or investments in front of you. There were two times in my life when I made investments that I thought would help me pivot toward Envisioning Prosperity. One felt pretty good. One didn't.

The one that felt pretty good was, in all honesty, low risk. About 1980, I was fresh out of Harvard Business School and penny stocks were all the rage. These were stocks that cost anywhere from a few cents to a couple of dollars per share. I wasn't really into them; frankly, I was focused on paying back my HBS school loans. But a guy I was dating at the time was very excited about one particular penny stock—Long Distance Discount Services, the company that became MCI and eventually Verizon. "Amy," he said. "This is the one! You've got to buy some. I've done the research. It's in telecommunications and it's going to blow up!" He was a CPA and was currently going through HBS, so he was no slouch. I took his advice and invested $500 in the company at a share price of not more than $1.25/share. Well, by 1982 that stock had blown up! (And, so had that relationship.) But with the proceeds of that stock purchase, I was able, with my soon-to-be husband, to make a significant down payment on our first home in Boston, during a time when interest rates were 11%. This enabled us to Envision Prosperity for sure. Our home was a lovely 2-unit building that looked like a private family house on a wide, tree-lined street. We had great tenants who paid us $800/month in rent, in cash and on time, every month. We certainly felt prosperous! We started our family there and enjoyed wonderful times with friends. The house grew in value, and we made a very nice profit when we moved to Minneapolis after my promotion to Director of Marketing for Lustrasilk, the company I helped Gillette acquire in 1986.

Have the Right Intentions for Prosperity

My career was doing well. Even though I had to turn down my dream job of working for Tom Burrell at his advertising agency in 1984 when I learned I was pregnant with our daughter, I was excited to become a marketing director. In retrospect, I can see I got a big head about it. My team had rebuilt the White Rain business, I helped acquire a company, was promoted—I wanted to pivot toward living a Vision of Prosperity that was commensurate with my title. It's at times like these when you really need to step back and ask, "What is your enough?" Well, I didn't ask myself that important question.

When we started looking at homes in Minneapolis, we met wonderful new friends courtesy of good friends from Boston who had moved there and introduced us around. They had beautiful homes around one of the lakes right in the city. When I saw that neighborhood, that was it—I wanted to live there, too. We also saw some truly lovely homes in the suburbs of Minneapolis. But I've never been a suburbanite—and I wanted what I wanted. That was totally *my* version of Envisioning Prosperity. When we were shown a big, beautiful home on a corner lot within walking distance of the premier lake in the city, I was smitten. The price was good. Almost too good—and that should have been a signal. It needed a bit of work—well, not really, but I wanted to turn the third floor into a fabulous master suite, and we had the proceeds to do it. I convinced my husband to go for it. For six months, I commuted from Boston to Minneapolis every two weeks to see my new baby and husband while I worked and had the renovations done. Or he brought the baby to see me. It was an absolutely crazy time. But we had a show-piece home when the work was done. We had a great time in that house. Lots of dinner parties and entertaining. Living the life.

Things were going well at the early days of my time at Lustrasilk. Sales were up, and the new products my team launched were taking off. The executive team from Gillette and the former owners of Lustrasilk got along well during the transition. So well, in fact, that one of the owners offered us "a great investment opportunity." As soon as he did, my internal gut reaction sensed that it was not something I should do. But did I listen? I think you know the answer. I was presented a prospectus full of positive information, which I studied thoroughly with my husband. He thought it had possibilities but was less than enthused. None of us were over the moon about the opportunity, but we decided to go for it. It was almost as if we were looking to do a deal in the spirit of good faith after the acquisition.

After the investment, it soon became clear that the promised returns were not going to be realized. The money invested was going to be a total loss. And it was not money that we as a family could really afford to lose. My tolerance for risk had failed me this time, and it was a tough pill to swallow. Needless to say, it was not a happy time in our household. Minneapolis, although a wonderful place with our cadre of close friends, was not very diverse. And during the winters, it was truly one of the coldest places I've ever lived in my life. When my husband applied to and was accepted to Northwestern's Kellogg School of Business in Chicago, I was ecstatic. I loved Chicago and couldn't wait to move there—yes, it had cold winters, but it was warmer than the 50 degrees below zero wind chill of Minneapolis during January. So, I wrote to Tom Burrell about finally coming to work for him. We put our beautiful home on the market, thinking it would be an easy sell.

That was not to be. Lesson: If you are Envisioning Prosperity with the wrong intentions or motivations, you may miss the signals along the road that are there to guide you toward what you really need. We missed, or ignored, the signal about the investment opportunity. Then we missed the signal about the good price for the size of the home. For one, we didn't recognize that the small apartment building right across the street from our home, on the block with other homes, would be a problem for buyers. Another was that our home was the nicest home on the block. It took a long time to sell that house. I learned a lot of real estate lessons from that Pivot toward Envisioning Prosperity.

That's another benefit from the 10 Pivot Points. While you won't always be successful, each Pivot Point will always teach you something, if you are open to the lessons. As a lifelong learner, I welcome the opportunity to find the lesson in every twist and turn on my journey.

Preparing to move to Chicago, it was time to look again for a home. This time, as my husband was in school, we choose to rent a home in Evanston, a suburb close to Northwestern, so he could more easily get to his classes. He had moved for me to Minneapolis, so this time I commuted into the city every day to work at Burrell, happy to finally be working for the legacy entrepreneurial firm and with the legendary Tom Burrell. It was a challenging time with two small children and a nanny to help manage, but somehow we did it. When my husband prepared to graduate, we needed to look for permanent housing. After two years in the suburbs, I was ready to live in the city and stop commuting. It was simply too hard to get to my children's activities from the city, or to my kids if they were ill. We looked hard and found a large vintage home in a historic South Side Chicago neighborhood at a reasonable price. No need for major renovations right away, just an upgrade of a bathroom would be needed down the road. Everything else was cosmetic. Or so I thought. The house had a wonderful wraparound front porch, five working fireplaces, a big backyard for the kids, great neighbors. It was easy for me to get to work, for my husband to get to his new job, and for the kids to be enrolled in good schools. Envisioning Prosperity was working, right?

When you think of prosperous people, the word affluence often comes to mind. The word affluence means "to flow." Well, it became apparent that soon after we moved into the house that my husband and I weren't flowing and had not been for some time. We separated, and it wasn't for the first time. After some difficult discussions and counseling, we made the decision to divorce. What things look like on the outside or how we present to the world may not be at all what things are like in reality. Some couples decide to stay together for the children. Our children knew something was amiss; we tried so hard to make things work. In the end, we made the decision to stay close to each other geographically for their sake, and that was a critical decision for their emotional well-being.

This was about 1995, the same time I started my consulting company as The Hilliard-Jones Marketing Group. That was already in motion. I went by the name of Amy Hilliard-Jones for many years once I got married. Pivoting through these major life changes really was a time to assess what Envisioning Prosperity meant.

The lesson from this time: During times of struggle, maintain what matters most to those who matter most to you. During that time, it was important to stay in the house for the kids so they could have their rooms, the backyard, and all their familiar surroundings. It helped that during that time our house was selected to be used in the now-classic movie *Love Jones*. I thought it was a joke when I got the notice in our mailbox from the Chicago Film Office. But it was real, and for over two weeks the stars of the film, the extras, the director, the crew, and all the teens in the neighborhood were at our house just having a ball! Everyone was terrific, the kids were excited, and I made a nice bit of money and had some bonus renovations done in the process. If you see the poster for the film with the cast in a home, or the scene at the party where Nia Long leaves the house after having arrived with Bill Bellamy and Larenz Tate follows her out, that was my house.

I maintained the home after our divorce in 1997, including putting on an entire new roof, repainting it, and upgrading that bathroom. When I put it on the market in 2000 to sell it to fund The ComfortCake Company, it sold quickly. I needed an office for The ComfortCake Company as I couldn't run it from home like I did with the consulting business. I found a loft office condo in an up-and-coming area called the South Loop near downtown Chicago and was able to negotiate a "rent with an option to buy" deal with no down payment. That worked very well for several years. The office was close to our frozen warehouse facility and key foodservice and retail customers, and it was a professional space where I could meet with banks, potential employees, and investors.

And yes, we were finally able to get a bank loan! I continued to Envision Prosperity for The ComfortCake Company. Monique Brinkman-Hill was a banker I first met in the early years of the business. We stayed in touch when she moved to ShoreBank, and she was instrumental in Envisioning Prosperity for The ComfortCake Company and getting us a SBA loan. She is a dear friend today, and I'll never forget her help. I kept Pivoting with Believing in Possibilities until I found a banker who also believed.

The loft office space was also great for media interviews where I could help utilize Pivot Point #10: Managing Perceptions. It was important for cultivating business for potential commercial customers and for our e-commerce customers to see us as a viable entity.

When the recession hit in 2008, however, the owner of the building decided to sell and asked if I wanted to buy the condo. That wasn't in my plans; my dad was ill, and my key supplier was pressuring me about slow payments. I looked at alternative spaces to move the business and didn't find anything suitable. It also was just too much to try and move the business at that time. In the end, I worked out a deal to buy the condo with a bank, keeping the mortgage payments slightly lower than the rent.

During this time, The ComfortCake Company was still doing well with the Chicago Public Schools. I was working hard to get other business, including for our patent-pending sugar-substitute, Sugarless Sweetness®. Sugarless Sweetness is a cup-for-cup granulated ingredient that was made for baking. Dad was a diabetic and kept eating too much ComfortCake at Thanksgiving. I told him he needed to stop, and he told me I needed to make a ComfortCake he could eat, and it had better taste as good as a regular one. As he was a World War II Air Force veteran, it was not really a request, so I said, "Yes, Sir!" I hired a food scientist to help me make an ingredient to swap out for sugar so I wouldn't have to change the commercial recipe. It took 18 months to do it, but it worked; we now license the ingredient to companies.

In 2009, we were able to secure a test with McDonald's in three markets. This was no small feat. The test did well, and we were very proud of that. Then McDonald's menu priorities changed and they did not pursue rolling out bakery items nationally, which was obviously quite disappointing. However, I have maintained good relationships there and you never know what may happen!

By 2011, though, things had gotten very tight for ComfortCake. Foodservice sales were down as the Chicago Public School menus were changing. Retail sales were slow due to distribution challenges and we had more bakery changes. My dad had passed; my mom was suffering from dementia and was staying with me during the summers. I had written countless proposals and made numerous presentations on Sugarless Sweetness, as I believed this was our key to real prosperity. Nothing big had come through, even though we had limited success with a line of sugarless cakes in Walmart and Potbelly restaurants. We even sold out of ComfortCake with Sugarless Sweetness on Home Shopping Network three times!

The highlight of 2012 was seeing my son, Nick, graduate Magna Cum Laude from Howard University, my alma mater. I am so very proud of him. That had been a goal for me when I started ComfortCake: seeing my two children get through college. As 2013 was coming to a close, however, it became clear that I needed to make some decisions about how I would Envision Prosperity. I had to make some major Pivots. It had become too difficult to maintain the profit margins in retail distribution with the contract manufacturing business model we had used from the beginning. To increase the retail profit margins, I would need to have my own food manufacturing plant. However, after researching this idea thoroughly, I decided against it. I knew enough about food manufacturing to know that I did not want to be responsible for keeping an entire plant full of orders or fixing the ovens if they broke down. In the end, I had to Re-Envision Prosperity for ComfortCake. I cut staff and focused on foodservice and e-commerce distribution only and stopped selling in retail stores.

The financial challenges during this time were significant. We had been selling Chicago Public Schools frozen batter and those profit margins were very different from the other items we sold them when the school menus changed. Even though we kept the volume, our cash flow was affected. This had an impact on our accounts payables. When this happens, it is vital to keep discussions open with suppliers, banks, landlords, and others with whom you do business, which we did. We worked out some arrangements, but in the end, I made the very tough decision to file personal bankruptcy at the end of 2013. This allowed me to maintain my home and keep the business afloat. Because of how I had always Envisioned Prosperity, filing for bankruptcy was something I could not talk about for years. A good friend of mine helped me get through that time by telling me, "Amy. Stop agonizing over this. You are using the tools that are there for situations just like this. And also, don't worry about what others may think. Most people *wish* they had your courage to go for their dreams like you did. And they are probably living paycheck to paycheck anyway!" That truly helped me press on.

Then the universe intervened. Linda Johnson Rice, the daughter of the founders of Johnson Publishing Company, which created *Ebony* and *Jet* magazines and Fashion Fair Cosmetics, and at the time was the largest company targeting women of color, called me toward the end of 2013. She said, "I know you have a food business, but would you consider coming over to Fashion Fair as president and running it?" My daughter, Angelica, said, "Mom, I'll run Comfort-Cake. Do it." So, I pivoted toward that opportunity, which allowed me to Envision Prosperity in a new light and continue Finding my Purpose and Believing in Possibilities.

I truly enjoyed much of my time leading Fashion Fair. It was a full circle moment for me, having met Mrs. Eunice Johnson, the creator of Fashion Fair 40 years earlier at a Halston fashion show in New York, where the Black models wore Fashion Fair makeup for the very first time. I felt I was helping keep that legacy alive, and it felt great being in a position to bring beauty to the African American market worldwide.

The benefits of the position also helped me financially with some of the business issues of The ComfortCake Company. I made the decision to sell the office condo and run the streamlined operations from my larger home condo as there was plenty of room there. Angelica did an awesome job of moving the business. Even so, some things are not in your control.

By 2016 it was clear that there were financial challenges at Johnson Publishing, which owned Fashion Fair. There had been many company-wide layoffs, and I became one of them. That was a first in my career and took some getting used to. But I had anticipated that something like that could happen, so I wasn't totally surprised. I had Shifted my Energy so I could Make my Moves.

I had quietly stopped manufacturing products from The ComfortCake Company at the beginning of 2016. We kept all our intellectual property intact: trademarks, patents, recipes. I shifted the company into licensing. I also had kept The Hillard Group (I eventually dropped the Jones) alive and well with speaking engagements and consulting contracts that didn't compete with Fashion Fair. In addition, I put my large condo on the market, as with just me there, it really was too much space. After renovating three homes, I was done with vintage living, and just wanted a more modern, down-sized space, hopefully with a view. I looked for an apartment to rent in earnest as I wasn't looking for another mortgage with condo assessment fees. I knew what my "enough" was by this time.

Wouldn't you know it—the universe stepped in again. In looking through the neighborhood paper for apartment listings, I saw a small ad for a "Three bedroom with lake and city views and wraparound terrace. Available now." And the picture was beautiful. I called to see if it was still available, and it was. I rushed right over. The empty apartment was serenely perfect. Long story short, I moved in a few months later. When I was viewing the apartment and measuring for my furniture, I kept wondering why the place felt so positive and serene. My friend Renee Ferguson, the award-winning investigative reporter, was with me and looked up the building. "Amy! This is Lester and Nancy McKeever's place!" The McKeevers used to own the 25-story apartment building I now live in. Lester McKeever is a prominent attorney, CPA, and was a partner in his own firm; he also served as chairman of the Federal Reserve Bank of Chicago. Nancy McKeever is a retired Chicago Public Schools teacher and former board chairman of the ETA Creative Arts Foundation. Nancy was one of the first people I met when I moved to Chicago to work for Tom Burrell. She was so gracious to me, introducing me to the community so I could volunteer to help others. And I worked with Lester on Mayor Richard M. Daley's 21st Century Planning Commission in the mid-1990s. I also know their daughter, Susan, and son, Steven. It is such a small world! It is an honor to live in the home they lived in for 40 years, and the building they purchased as the first African American owners of a high-rise property in Chicago.

And my former condo? Because the condo and the vintage building it was in needed work, it took a long time to sell and eventually went into foreclosure. I had to let the feelings about that go, too. Yet the Pivot of Envisioning Prosperity again prevailed as a good friend was able to buy the condo, loves it, and I'm thrilled that her family is enjoying it.

PIVOT

Prosperity Is in the Eye of the Beholder

Writing this chapter was one of the most profound to relive. Profound because by going back over the times when I thought I was prosperous in life, people and circumstances taught me what Envisioning Prosperity really meant. When I Pivoted to the true meaning of Envisioning Prosperity for me, my life became so much more satisfying, authentic, and real. I am living with what I need versus what I thought I wanted, and that truth is worth its weight in gold.

Here are the key lessons in Envisioning Prosperity:

- Always Know Thyself. However, you change over time. Don't beat yourself up as you find your true vision of prosperity.
- Ask yourself, "What is my enough?" What is enough to let you enjoy life and not worry about how to make it month to month? A big house can be pretty to look at, but the bills to keep it up may not be pretty at all.

- Are you making a living or making a life? Have you thought about the difference? Give yourself time to be reflective and spend that time wisely. Time is not replaceable. Money is.
- How do your children, family, and friends feel about you now as you Envision Prosperity? What do they mean to you, and you to them?
- Is building a legacy important to you? Giving back to your community? Those things can make you feel very prosperous.

Part II: Shift Your Energy

5

Getting Prepared

Like the company DreamWorks®, you have to work to live your dreams.

IN THE PREVIOUS chapters, the Pivot Points ask you to do a lot of inner work—in service of Honing Your Vision—and you are asked to be intentional and specific. Now it's time to Shift Your Energy and get even more specific and detailed in your plans. Whatever stage you are in—whether you've just recognized what you want to do, or you're ready to write a full business plan for your new endeavors—it is time to put pen to paper and Get Prepared.

The best way to think of this Pivot Point is to tap into your passion and direct it into goals and steps that will take you toward your desired outcome. This dovetails perfectly with why I placed the Getting Prepared Pivot Point ahead of Honoring Your Passion (#8). Far too often, people come up to me with passionate ideas and a request: *Tell me what to do to accomplish my dream.* Passion is critical to have, and inspiring to hear, but doing the work is nonnegotiable. In any field of endeavor, professionals who are masters of their crafts prepare—and prepare hard. And they prepare in an aligned sequence so that the tasks are done at the appropriate time and not in a haphazard way.

Getting Prepared Gives You a Framework

I recently watched *Dance Dreams* on Netflix, a documentary about dancer, choreographer, actor, director, producer, and writer Debbie Allen. It tells not only of her life story, but of how each year she brings to life her unique take on the classic *The Nutcracker* ballet. She turned the concept into the *Hot Chocolate Nutcracker*, performed by young dancers from the Debbie Allen Dance Academy in Los Angeles. It was truly a master class in preparation. You may be familiar with Debbie Allen from the *Fame* television show and movie, or *Grey's Anatomy*, where she acts, directs, and executive produces. But dancing is in her DNA and her training from that permeates everything she does. Debbie is an example of someone who uses the first five Pivot Points exceptionally well for her dance academy, which is a nonprofit enterprise. Following are Debbie Allen's Pivot Points:

- She Found Her Purpose—to bring professional dance techniques to those who may not have that opportunity.
- She Believes in Possibilities that her dance academy could be created and sustained, and through her fierce advocacy, inspires others to believe also.
- Her Priorities are well defined—to create and teach the programs and continue raising the funds to stay viable.
- She Envisions Prosperity as culturally enriching the lives of young people.
- And boy, does she put her students, herself, and her team through the rigors of Getting Prepared! She expects her young dancers to be on time, to practice hard, and to be professional at all times. She expects herself and her team to understand the difference between being prepared and planning.

In one of her blog posts, life coach Laurie Dupar gives a unique and important distinction between preparation and planning: "Preparation does more than prepare you for what to expect; it puts you in a position to handle what you didn't see coming."[1] She goes on to say, "Planning leads to awareness, preparation leads to readiness."

I agree. It's this kind of thinking that is built into Pivot Point #5. Getting Prepared is about developing a **framework** for your plans. A framework allows for time to think about what happens if Plan A doesn't work. What would Plan B look like? When shifting your energy to pivot toward a new life direction, Getting Prepared can start by simply taking out a crisp new notebook and writing your dream on page one. Then create what I call a "Reverse Calendar": Write down today's date. Then write down the goal date—6 months or a year from now, whatever your target date—for where you'd like to be after you make your move to pivot. It could be your store grand opening, making your first million, a key priority you've Defined in Pivot Point #3, leaving lots of space in between. Next, put down the months between those dates. Quickly, put down three key things you need to do each month to meet your goal. Get your mind prepared but *write it down*! That is the start of your Plan A framework. Then, do the same for a Plan B framework. With those two Reverse Calendars, you have started Getting Prepared enough to begin putting some specific plans in place.

By doing this your mind will start moving you to *action*. Instead of being stuck in the fantasy of your dream, you'll be Shifting Your Energy from Believing in Possibilities (#1) to making them a reality. As you get more specific with your planning, it's important to review your plans on a regular basis to keep yourself prepared. It will help your focus, reduce your stress, and identify options. This way,

---

[1] Laurie Dupar, "Why Preparation, Not Planning, Is the Key to Success," ADHD Strategies blog (Sept. 1, 2017), https://www.iactcenter.com/adhd-blog/strategies/preparation-not-planning-key-success/

when the inevitable Murphy's Law kicks in, you will be trained to pivot to move on quickly to the next way to move ahead.

As a serial entrepreneur with more than my share of side hustles, I use the Reverse Calendar tool often. It has helped me make my ideas become very real. It also prioritizes my ideas with my values and resources. I also used this Pivot Point when seeking a new career path, job project or promotion, or educational move. I suspect you can even use this Pivot Point of Getting Prepared to find a life partner! I know that some people are just that intentional—I will have to try it (smile). That's the beauty of the 10 Pivot Points. You can focus them on all aspects of your life, from business to personal.

By the time I left Harvard Business School, I no longer had the dream of running my own retail store. My time spent in a retail environment cooled that dream for me. Even though I was sure my own store would have been less hectic, at the time it did not seem like a path that would Envision the Prosperity that HBS had positioned in my mind. I had begun my love of marketing while I was a first-year student at Harvard. I was inspired by Professor Steve Starr. He had boundless energetic *joy* about marketing as he circled the tiered classroom teaching us in his booming voice. But he was dead serious about making sure we got the fundamentals. At Harvard, classes were taught by the Socratic method, all in case studies. You could be called on without notice to present to the class the assigned case for the day, and your classmates would then try to tear apart your analysis. I always sat in the front of the class so I would not miss anything. Early in my first year, Professor Starr called on me. "Miss Hilliard," he bellowed, "you are the vice president of the Acme Paint Company. Sales are down. What are you going to do?" With my knees shaking under the desk, in my most confident "I'm from Detroit and Howard University" voice, I said, "I am going to raise the advertising budget by $5 million so that people know we make the best paint in America!" Then, I proceeded to lay out the case successfully. From that point on, I was hooked, and I wanted a summer job at a big ad agency in New York.

Professor Starr became my mentor, and we developed a framework for getting me a job by the summer. We worked out what to do month by month to get to my goal of a job by June, using what became the model for a Reverse Calendar. And the mindset of Getting Prepared was key, because in 1977 most of the big agencies didn't have summer intern programs for MBA students. So, I had to have Plans A, B, C, D, and more down the alphabet. Finally, with the help of referral letters from Professor Starr, Frank Mingo of J. Walter Thompson, and Carolyn Jones of BBDO, Young and Rubicam (Y&R), the largest ad agency on Madison Avenue, created a summer internship for me. From the fall through the spring as I Pivoted and Got Prepared, I Honed My Vision in on Y&R. Marie Mandry, the VP of HR, had answered my letter graciously, and we were off to the races. While they didn't have a program, we created one together, based on how I could help them, what I'd learn, and what we could structure for a future intern program. It was everything I hoped it would be. My love for marketing, reinforced through this internship and my experiences at HBS, was the catalyst for me to Find My (New) Purpose and Hone My Vision for what I wanted.

A Reverse Calendar may seem like Gantt charts often used in business to map out major team projects by department, person, and due dates. Conceptually, it is. But it is a lot less detailed, and sometimes, make that many times, it is the best way to light a creative spark, get unstuck, or to get the ball rolling for your team. I used this to get the team moving on White Rain Shampoo when we only had six months to get a new product on the shelves. Each member filled in the specifics for their areas of expertise, and then we had a plan.

The Reverse Calendar also really works for side hustles. While at Gillette, I still had a toe in the fashion world, as people kept asking me for fashion tips. This was in the early 1980s when fashion took an interest in the professional woman's wardrobe. I was never interested

in wearing the blue suit and little paisley tie look that was being promoted. So, to make extra money for Christmas one spring I laid out
a framework for a wardrobe consulting business for working women.
I called it *Appointments*. I wanted it to be taken seriously by women
who could afford to pay me $50 an hour. I did a Reverse Calendar
that would put me in business by the end of the summer when women
would want to update their wardrobes for the fall season. I had my
good friend in Gillette's graphics department design wonderful business cards and a brochure for me, I identified potential clients, stores
to shop in, and voilà! I was on my way and had a nice cushion for
Christmas gifts. I didn't need a full-fledged business plan, because I
could see from that "market test" that while a good concept, *Appointments* would be hard for me to scale.

Years later, I looked at buying Bob the Chef's soul food restaurant in Boston, one of the most popular places in town. In that
instance, the Reverse Calendar framework was critical in identify-
ing the specifics needed for that major undertaking. That project
involved not only buying and operating the restaurant, but it came
with a multi-unit rental property. My husband and I looked very
seriously at that deal and came close to making it happen. When
the Reverse Calendar indicated we needed to investigate the tax
situation as part of our due diligence, some things came to light
that gave us pause. We could have pressed on, but we decided not
to. Because of that early bullet point on our Reverse Calendar, in
our conversations with the owner, we discovered those concerning
issues sooner; without that, it might have taken longer to discover
or may not have come to light in time to pull out of the deal. This
is an example of how Getting Prepared is not the same as planning.
It is a mindset that helps your planning.

When directing teams of people, Getting Prepared is a vital
part of planning. This is important no matter the environment. I've
renovated three vintage properties. To get the best work out of the
general contractors, especially on the renovation I did while I was
commuting between Boston and Minneapolis with a six-month-old

baby to care for, my Reverse Calendar kept me focused on when that project had to be completed. It was much easier to keep things on pace and hold the contractors accountable by itemizing what key things needed to be completed by what months. The last thing I needed was to bring my young baby into a house filled with construction dust. My spiral notebooks of Reverse Calendars may have looked like school books, but trust me, they were all about business.

The same was true after I sold my home to start The Comfort-Cake Company. The condo I bought for my family to live in needed a total renovation—at the same time I was starting the business. Yes, I am a Type A person. Know Thyself. Get Prepared. I could have bought a smaller place, surely, or one that didn't need so much work. But I had used Pivot Point #3 and Defined My Priorities. My children gave up a lot for me to sell our big house on the South Side of Chicago. I did not want them cramped in a small place just as they were entering junior and senior high school. I wanted them to have a space where they could easily bring their friends. In fact, it was a conscious decision to have a place where their friends, especially my son's friends, would *want* to hang out so that I and their parents would know where they were. We lived in the city of Chicago and keeping our boys close was important. Those Reverse Calendars were on hand at all times as I supervised the renovation work, the commercialization of my recipes for my new company, along with the packaging development, sales, operations, hiring, everything. Not that I did it alone. I was very fortunate to have a wonderful office manager at ComfortCake, Claudine Jordan, otherwise known as the erstwhile and always efficient Cj. Cj and I were together a long time. She was my assistant at Burrell Communications, The Hilliard Group, Soft Sheen, and eventually followed me to Fashion Fair Cosmetics. Cj was an excellent example of Pivot Point #7, Seeking Positivity, as well.

Lesson: Frameworks also help keep the main things the *main things*. As a leader, you cannot possibly keep all the details in your mind. The most successful and experienced leaders understand that.

It's a lesson micromanagers (hey, I've been that too at times!) must learn. Pivoting to a Getting Prepared mindset allows your team to take more ownership of the details. Yes, there are times you may need to get in the weeds. Been there, done that. But those frameworks can keep you from being overwhelmed when you have to sweat the small stuff.

Getting Prepared Is a Mindset

Let me talk about how pivoting to a Getting Prepared mindset can help you in securing the big stuff. Here's a snapshot of some of the companies I've worked for, clients serviced, and customers served:

Bloomingdale's	McDonald's
Young & Rubicam	Walmart
Gillette/Lustrasilk	7-Eleven
Mary Kay Cosmetics	Home Shopping Network
Pillsbury	United Airlines
Burrell Communications	Walgreen's
L'Oréal/Soft Sheen	Safeway
American Express	Aetna
IBM	Hallmark
HBO	Coca-Cola
Ford Motor Company	Black Entertainment Television (BET)
PepsiCo	Nielsen
The Gap	Target
Pandora Jewelry	Fortune Magazine

I share this to paint a picture of how a Getting Prepared mindset helped me to align with the "big boys." I had to elevate my mind to seek out the top companies to build my résumé and entrepreneurial portfolio with credibility. These companies have immediate name recognition in most halls of business and with most consumers. To Pivot my experience with them into leverage was vital as I developed sales proposals, wrote investment briefs, applied for commercial loans, and moved into bigger jobs. Do you need to go to Harvard Business School to have this kind of mindset? Absolutely not. Research is free. I did the work, and you can too. I always research the companies I desire to align with, to best position what I can offer to them. What were their strategic plans, how were they doing in the marketplace, how could I add value? Creating value for others is one of the most important parts of Getting Prepared. How are you going to create value for others as you develop the plans to meet you own goals? As you Get Prepared to align with others, understand that they are tuned in to radio station WIFM—"WHAT'S IN IT FOR ME?" Never lose sight of this as you write your proposal, plan, and make your pitch. If you do so, you are halfway home. Well, perhaps not halfway, but I've found if you keep that radio station in mind, you can keep people more interested in what you have to offer.

Getting Prepared also involves sales. Yes, SALES. You may be thinking, I'm an engineer or accountant or an artist or a mother. I'm not in sales. Yes. You. Are. If you are in any facet of business or management, professionally or personally, you have to sell to someone. You have to do the work of convincing others that your idea, project, invention, air force carrier, or Brussels sprouts are good for them. I counsel people in professions outside of sales to read books about the selling profession. There are many, so again, do the research to find one that resonates for you. You do not have to become a salesperson, but you do have to become skilled in the mindset of selling. As you do your research, you may be surprised at the number of CEOs who come from a sales background. It's knowing the *framework* of selling that counts. The bottom line is creating value. You demonstrate that value by showing your customer you know their business better than they do.

If you are considering full-time entrepreneurship, there are some special considerations as you Pivot to Getting Prepared. Unless you are faced with a situation that propels you into entrepreneurship suddenly (such as unexpectedly taking over a business or losing your job), taking the time to Pivot and Get Prepared for this challenging and at times exhilarating period of life is key.

I was the SVP of Marketing at L'Oréal/Soft Sheen for two years. The idea for The ComfortCake Company came while I was there and as I considered leaving L'Oréal/Soft Sheen to start this new business, I took a hard look at my finances. I cleared up my credit cards. I stopped buying unnecessary clothes and other items for myself and my household. I started saving money to support us while ComfortCake got off the ground. I also looked at my time and where I was spending it. I prioritized my volunteer work, knowing my time would become limited once I started the business. Fortunately, I had built up a lot of goodwill in the community in the past. Once ComfortCake got started, I donated samples for community events to support good causes, pivoting the contributions I could make in lieu of time for my volunteer work.

It was also important to look at my health. You have to eat your Wheaties *every* day as an entrepreneur to deal with the stresses that can come from building your own business. It is still a priority for me to get enough exercise and eat healthy foods. You also must prepare your family. For me, I prepared my family not to expect annual big vacations like we had when I was in the corporate world. That was hard for them and for me. Travel is something we all love and still do. Part of Getting Prepared is to have clear communications with those close to you about how life will change so that expectations can be managed. Even your friends need to understand that your time will not be as accessible. At the same time, do not cut people off, as you will need them for support when you hit those bumps in the road. Relationships matter.

So, you have done a Reverse Calendar. Gotten your house in order. You're ready to go into sales mode and sell. You are doing research as you prepare to do a business plan. Take a moment to step back before you jump in deeper. Do you know yourself? This is another important aspect of this Pivot Point. As you are about to make a Pivot toward a new direction, whether it's your own business, new job, a move across the country, or another major challenge, look inward and assess if you have what it takes to Make the Move. As you Hone Your Vision and Shift Your Energy, a valuable thing to have in place is your personal board of directors. These are people in your life who know you, whom you respect, and who will tell you the truth. Tell them about your plans. Ask them what they think. A personal board of directors can be critical advisors at key points in your life. If you don't have one, I strongly recommend you build one, and nurture those relationships, as they are vital for the pivot of Getting Prepared.

As I said earlier, people often come to me with passionate ideas and ask for my help in getting them off the ground. I try to be encouraging, but I am direct and ask if they have done a business plan. That is that last part of Getting Prepared I want to cover in this chapter. I will not do a full-court press on how to write a business plan; there are many books available on that subject. What I will provide here is a basic framework for you to consider as you think about your passion that you'd like to bring to life. Everyone won't be as lucky as the Southwest Airlines cofounder Herb Kelleher, who, legend has it, wrote his business plan on a cocktail napkin in a San Antonio restaurant. But with a framework of what it takes to write a plan to start a business, you can keep the primary components in mind as you consider your opportunity.

As you Get Prepared and work toward creating a business plan, having the framework of one in mind (and written down) as you work through your Reverse Calendar helps keep Your Vision Honed as you continue on the path to making your dreams real. The Small Business Association has a good framework for a business plan:[2]

Executive Summary

Briefly tell your reader what your company is and why it will be successful. Include your mission statement, your product or service, and basic information about your company's leadership team, employees, and location. You should also include financial information and high-level growth plans if you plan to ask for financing.

Company Description

Use your company description to provide detailed information about your company. Go into detail about the problems your business solves. Be specific, and list out the consumers, organization, or businesses your company plans to serve.

Explain the competitive advantages that will make your business a success. Are there experts on your team? Have you found the perfect location for your store? Your company description is the place to boast about your strengths.

Market Analysis

You'll need a good understanding of your industry outlook and target market. Competitive research will show you what other businesses are doing and what their strengths are. In your market research, look for trends and themes. What do successful competitors do? Why does it work? Can you do it better? Now's the time to answer these questions.

---

[2]U.S. Small Business Administration, Business Guide: Plan Your Business, Write Your Business Plan, Traditional Business Plans, SBA website, https://www.sba.gov/business-guide/plan-your-business/write-your-business-plan

Organization and Management

Tell your reader how your company will be structured and who will run it.

Describe the <u>legal structure</u> of your business. State whether you have or intend to incorporate your business as a C or an S corporation, form a general or limited partnership, or if you're a sole proprietor or LLC.

Use an organizational chart to lay out who's in charge of what in your company. Show how each person's unique experience will contribute to the success of your venture. Consider including résumés and CVs of key members of your team.

Service or Product Line

Describe what you sell or what service you offer. Explain how it benefits your customers and what the product life cycle looks like. Share your plans for intellectual property, like copyright or patent filings. If you're doing <u>research and development</u> for your service or product, explain it in detail.

Marketing and Sales

There's no single way to approach a marketing strategy. Your strategy should evolve and change to fit your unique needs.

Your goal in this section is to describe how you'll attract and retain customers. You'll also describe how a sale will actually happen. You'll refer to this section later when you make financial projections, so make sure to thoroughly describe your complete marketing and sales strategies.

Funding Request

If you're asking for funding, this is where you'll outline your funding requirements. Your goal is to clearly explain how much you'll need over the next five years and what you'll use it for.

Specify whether you want debt or equity, the terms you'd like applied, and the length of time your request will cover. Give a detailed description of how you'll use your funds. Specify if you need funds to buy equipment or materials, pay salaries, or cover specific bills until revenue increases. Always include a description of your future strategic financial plans, such as paying off debt or selling your business.

Financial Projections

Supplement your funding request with financial projections. Your goal is to convince the reader that your business is stable and will be a financial success.

If your business is already established, include income statements, balance sheets, and cash flow statements for the last three to five years. If you have other collateral you could put against a loan, make sure to list it now.

Provide a prospective financial outlook for the next five years. Include forecasted income statements, balance sheets, cash flow statements, and capital expenditure budgets. For the first year, be even more specific and use quarterly—or even monthly—projections. Make sure to clearly explain your projections and match them to your funding requests.

Appendix

Use your appendix to provide supporting documents or other materials that were specially requested. Common items to include are credit histories, résumés, product pictures, letters of reference, licenses, permits, or patents, legal documents, permits, and other contracts.

P⬆⬇VOT

Getting Prepared Is a Mindset for the Foundation of Your Plans

What I hope you have learned from Pivot Point #5 is that to develop the best plans to Shift Your Energy, your mind has to be in the right place. To get there, you need to get out of your head, and write things down. Not the business plan first, but your steps toward putting it together.

Here are the key lessons from Getting Prepared:

- Honoring Your Passion is important but Getting Prepared is vital
- Constructing a Reverse Calendar on paper can help your dreams become real
- Frameworks help keep the main thing the *main thing*
- Know Thyself Always, particularly when taking on multiple projects
- Secure a personal board of directors who will tell you the truth
- Everyone sells by creating value for others

6

Having Patience

Putting one foot in front of the other is the only way to create a path.

I MUST ADMIT, of the 10 Pivot Points, this one is the most challenging for me. In the many stages of my life where I had to Hone My Vision to Find my Purpose, Believe in Possibilities, Define My Priorities, and Envision prosperity for myself, I was able to Shift My Energy. I have hunkered down, Gotten Prepared—and then had to *wait* for things to happen. As a true Type A person, I like to see things happen with a quickness. I love results. And yet, most often it takes time for things to align, even when you have made the decision to strategically Pivot in a new direction. When I reflect on many of the formative experiences I've had in my professional life, I realize that despite wanting things to happen quickly, some of my greatest successes have come because I was patient for the right moment to present itself.

Patience is defined in the Oxford Dictionary as "the capacity to accept or tolerate delay, trouble or suffering without getting angry or upset." According to *Psychology Today*, you can transcend frustration with patience, and patience is not passivity or resignation, but **power**.[1] The article goes on to say it's an emotionally freeing practice of waiting, watching, and knowing when to act. I really liked that.

Developing patience is a very useful skill. This time of waiting can be very productive. It can strengthen your emotional management muscles, as you must learn to respond to events, not just react to them. By taking the time to respond, you can step back and make better decisions. In doing so, untold opportunities may be discovered. An *Inc.* magazine article titled "17 Quotes About the Remarkable Power of Patience" recently shared perspectives about Having Patience, especially in today's times of instant gratification. We are in a microwave society where we want immediate responses to texts, calls, proposals, and more. Yet, as the article stated, "Sometimes the best things in life are the things we wait the longest for."[2] That really resonates with me as to why Having Patience is a Pivot Point. It makes me remember the untold number of times in my life where Having Patience was crucial to achieving my goals. Why? Because Having Patience allows me to step back and reassess circumstances, facts, timing, experience, and align my emotions so I can more effectively Shift My Energy to make my best moves.

When I was a junior at Howard University, many of my fellow classmates were preparing to go on to law school, medical school, or business school. Dean Milton Wilson of Howard's Business School had taken an interest in me, and suggested I apply to business school to get my MBA. I hadn't really thought about it as something I might do after graduation. I was focused on becoming

[1]Judith Orloff, M.D., "The Power of Patience," *Psychology Today* (Sept. 18, 2012), https://www.psychologytoday.com/us/blog/emotional-freedom/201209/the-power-patience
[2]Peter Economy, "17 Quotes About the Remarkable Power of Patience," *Inc.* (Oct. 8, 2018), https://www.inc.com/peter-economy/17-quotes-about-remarkable-power-of-patience.html

a retail fashion buyer. He told me I could still do that, but with the MBA degree, I'd have many more options down the road.

So, I started looking into getting an MBA and researching schools with my buddies. Most of my ambitious buddies were guys in the Liberal Arts Student Council, and they were all going to law school. One of them, Geoff Simmons, gave me some of the best advice of my career: "Amy, always start at the top. Apply to the top schools first. If they say no, then go to the next tier down. But one of the top tier schools may say yes! You'll never know if you don't try them first." That philosophy has stayed with me forever. Apply to the top first. Believe in Possibilities. Thank you, Geoff. He and I are still friends today. And of course, he's a successful lawyer!

I took Geoff's advice and applied to the top ten graduate business schools in the country. Harvard, Columbia, Wharton, Stanford, and the others. My grades were good; my recommendation letters, stellar; yet I didn't have much math in my background, so the more numbers-oriented schools took a pass. But . . . I will never forget receiving that letter in the mail from the Harvard Business School. I was so excited, I called my parents and read it to them as I read it for the first time: "Dear Amy, You have been accepted to the Harvard Business School's graduating class of 1978." Wait, what??? I was graduating from Howard in May 1974. I expected to go to grad school that fall, attending a two-year program—and that meant graduating from HBS in 1976. What Harvard had given me was a "Deferred Admit." The letter went on. "We feel you will be a great asset to HBS. Given your background, we are offering you a deferred admission to allow you to work for two years to strengthen your experience and we also require you to take a pre-calculus course to better prepare you for the course work ahead." I was **devastated** and could *not* believe it!! I was not patient at all. My parents had to tell me to calm down, stop crying, and think things through.

I took several deep breaths. I **had** to Pivot. My first realization: I HAD GOTTEN INTO HARVARD BUSINESS SCHOOL!!! But I would need to Have Patience and put in more work before heading to Boston. Now my vision for the next two years suddenly became crystal clear. I needed a job that would give me good experience. And I had to Shift My Energy to do that. Until I did that, I couldn't start making moves.

Patience Can Unlock the Door to Dreams

The Harvard Business School acceptance came by the Christmas break of my senior year at Howard. Since I was fully anticipating going to grad school, I hadn't really started a job search. Now I had to go into full-court press to get a job, and not just any job. Having had success with the "Start with the Top" approach in applying to grad school, I used that same approach to search for a job—apply to the top jobs I wanted and go from there.

Bloomingdale's was the #1 department store in the country at the time. The Queen of England had just made a visit to the flagship store in New York City, for goodness' sake! Given that I wanted a career in retail fashion buying, I knew I had to apply there. I did, and as backup, I also applied to Hudson's in Detroit, and other major stores in the country. But "Bloomie's" was my first choice by far. I also applied to Polaroid—not in retail fashion buying, obviously— but where I had worked at an awesome summer job. From that summer job, I maintained good contacts there and already had a good reputation. I knew it could serve as a backup plan. Importantly and strategically, all my options were blue-chip companies. The "Top Approach" eventually morphed into a lifelong résumé-building strategy that has served me well.

That approach, and Having Patience as I waited to hear back, served me well at this time, too. I got offers from Bloomingdale's, Hudson's, and Polaroid. Hudson's and Polaroid came after me hard with higher monetary offers. But my vision, mind, and heart were set on Bloomingdale's, and after making it past the on-campus interviews, off I went to New York for further interviews to determine which department I'd work in. In New York, the HR department had interviews set up in the Men's department—socks and ties— telling me that was a good place for a new retail buying trainee to start. "Hmmm," I thought. "That doesn't sound like much fun." As I was waiting, the HR manager came back with more paperwork for me. Believing in Possibilities, here was my chance, and I was going to take it. I humbly asked her, "Since I'm here in New York, can I at least have an 'exploratory interview' with the buyer of the Designer Dress department?" I figured, what did I have to lose? I remembered to go for the TOP. The HR manager must have known the buyer, because she made a quick call. The next thing I knew, I was sent up to the office of Miss Elaine Monroe, the buyer of Place Elegante, *the* Designer Dress department of Bloomingdale's. I'm talking Halston. Givenchy. Bill Blass. Oscar de la Renta. Anne Klein. Valentino. *The Top of the Top.* Miss Monroe, as she always told me to call her, and I got along great. She made a call back to the HR manager, and basically said, "I don't care what policy says, I want Amy to work for me. Make it happen." And that was that. Wow! Instead of jumping at the first assignment offered just to get started at Bloomingdale's, Having Patience kicked in at precisely the right time. I had the patience to wait a beat and ask for what I wanted. Socks and ties in the Men's department was not where I wanted to be at Bloomingdale's. It was risky. I somehow knew I needed to have patience, to take that breath to find the right moment, and make it known what I was most interested in. It was also a lesson about asking for "exploratory" interviews, meetings, calls, etc. Using the word "exploratory" eases the pressure on the person who has the power to make something happen for you. It really is a Having Patience strategy because it is a more indirect approach of putting your ideas on the table. This has worked successfully for me my entire career.

I had not just landed a job at Bloomingdale's, I had *the job I wanted* at Bloomingdale's. Making this happen after having no job prospects at Christmas break took most of the spring semester. I secured my dream job in April, returned to campus, finished my coursework, and graduated from Howard in May 1974. After graduation, I packed my belongings in my yellow Volkswagen Beetle and drove to New York City. To this day I remember seeing Manhattan come into view as I drove over the George Washington Bridge. I was on top of the world.

The next Monday I reported for work in the most beautiful area of retail I'd ever seen in a department store. Mirrors, delicate displays, and dresses worth thousands of dollars. And the clientele . . . Betsy Bloomingdale herself. Jackie Onassis. Diana Ross. Babe Paley, wife of legendary CBS boss Bill Paley. All the New York socialites. And me! In those first months, I helped pick out the clothes they would buy, attended all the fashion shows on Seventh Avenue in the famous showrooms. I had a total blast! I went to parties at Calvin Klein's apartment. I paid as much for one pair of Valentino trousers as a full month's rent (and wore those pants for 10 years until they fell apart). I danced all night at disco hot spots. I rode my bike down Second Avenue from Harlem to Wall Street early on Saturday mornings. My gay buddies taught me how to walk the catwalk as I was trying to be a model in my spare time and getting my portfolio done.

I learned so many valuable lessons those two years in New York City. Let's start with my job. Working at Bloomingdale's was like working on Broadway, where the curtain would rise, and the play would start every single day. The audience—our customers—had no idea what was going on backstage: the mayhem, making sure the floor was merchandised perfectly, the deliveries from all over the world, stock counts, racks of clothes zooming by at the speed of light. Literally, it was theater, and I was learning it from the masters. And the quality of the couture clothing was the best in the world. I learned how to tell by looking at items from the inside out. Miss Monroe patiently taught me, making sure that the items we ordered matched the samples we ordered from. Important lessons.

I had a high level of responsibility for someone right out of college, including helping to manage the sales staff. Place Elegante was a commission-only department. The sales ladies had been there for years, and each had a "book" with their clientele, but the competition for sales could be brutal. These ladies were much, much older than I was, and I was the only African American in the entire department. I had to win their respect and trust. To do so, I focused on being professional, looking professional, being pleasant to work with, asking their opinions, learning from them, and applying the appropriate Pivot Point for Success to win them over. And I did. Having Patience played a key role. Each day, I took time to patiently talk and get to know the sales ladies. We'd talk about their lives, likes, and best sales skills so I could know them as people, and they could know me. Importantly, as they got to know me, they saw they could trust me. Building trust takes time and Having Patience was essential.

One of the most unforgettable moments of my time at Bloomingdale's came early in my employment. It was the height of Fashion Week, and all of Seventh Avenue was buzzing with the fashion shows. Miss Monroe and I were going to attend Halston's show one afternoon—the top American designer of the time. She was running late and sent me ahead to get our seats. I scurried off to the showroom. When I arrived at the main door, letting them know I was there for the show, I was promptly told, "Deliveries are in the back." Knowing my value, I patiently stood tall, squared my shoulders, looked the showroom person in the eye, and said, "I'm Amy Hilliard, Miss Elaine Monroe's assistant buyer from Bloomingdale's, and I believe our seats are in the front." Well, that person quickly ushered me into a front-row seat in the packed showroom.

Miss Monroe hadn't arrived yet, and the show hadn't started, when an elegantly dressed and bejeweled African American woman promptly came right over to me and said, "Young lady, you are sitting in the front row of Halston's show and I don't know who you are." I knew *exactly* who she was. "Mrs. Johnson!" I declared. "What an honor to meet you! I know who you are!" Mrs. Eunice Johnson was married to John H. Johnson, and they owned *Ebony* and *Jet* magazines. Every year Mrs. Johnson put on the renowned Ebony

Fashion Fair touring fashion show in at least 25 major US cities, featuring couture fashions she bought from top designers in New York, Paris, and Milan. She was a very important customer in the fashion world. That day, as we waited for Halston's show to begin, I explained that I was the assistant buyer from Bloomingdale's. Mrs. Johnson said to me, "Well young lady, that's wonderful. I'm glad you're here, because you will see history today. Every one of the Black models on the runway will be wearing Fashion Fair Cosmetics for the very first time. We are launching our own line of cosmetics for women of color because none of the big cosmetic companies would do it. Our models always had to mix and match shades during our fashion shows. We asked Charles Revson, Helena Rubenstein, and Max Factor to make darker shades for our community, but they wouldn't, so Mr. Johnson and I did it ourselves." Little did I know how that moment would come full circle 40 years later when I would become president of Fashion Fair Cosmetics.

I loved much about my job at Bloomingdale's. The thrill of opening up the first Valentino boutique in the country within Place Elegante and having Valentino himself sell me a pair of his designer grey flannel pants in his intoxicating Italian accent. "Bellissima, Ameee!! You simply must have them!" I was also able to bring the concept of Supplier Diversity to Bloomingdale's in my own small way. My dear and talented friend from Detroit, Claude Payne, was trying to make it as a fashion designer in New York. Within his collection of exquisite dresses, he had some designs I thought Miss Monroe should see, so I got him an appointment. She bought a dozen of the dresses—and they sold out! Claude was on his way and I couldn't have been more proud.

I worked extremely hard. Back then, the buying staff not only had to buy the clothes and manage the sales staff, but they also had total responsibility for merchandising the floor. This meant going to the shipping rooms daily to accurately check in our department's deliveries, managing getting the merchandise from the shipping rooms to the department floor (otherwise known as "schlepping the racks"), taking inventory, and working 12-hour days at least twice a week when the store would be open until 9 p.m. As exciting as it was, it was also grueling. My dreams of being a fashion retail buyer soon met with the reality of doing so within a large department store environment. And while working, I was also taking pre-calculus courses to get ready for Harvard. In all honestly, my patience was wearing a bit thin thinking about doing this type of work for two full years.

Knowing I was ultimately going to Harvard, I wondered if there was another way to stay in fashion but not do it under such hard, physically draining circumstances. I could keep learning about the business, I thought, and if I had my own store one day, I wouldn't have to work such long hours. Fortunately, in my showroom rounds on Seventh Avenue, I met and became friendly with Kitty Hart, the head of Designer Direction for the May Company Department Stores buying office. The May Company had no stores in New York and depended on their buying office to preview all the designer lines and write up the best suggestions so that the buyers would use their time wisely when they came to New York on buying trips. Kitty needed an assistant and told me to let her know if I ever wanted to leave Bloomingdale's. Whoa! A buying office job was 9 to 5. No inventory taking. No schlepping racks. Still going to fashion shows. Now that sounded like a great way reinvigorate Having Patience about having to work the two full years and still be able to stay in the fashion business. So, I shifted my energy, made a Pivot, and took the May Company job. I left Bloomingdale's on good terms.

The move proved to be a good one. I learned another side of the business, including the different part of fashion merchandising writing skills. I also had the time to pursue my dream of trying to become a model myself. Once my portfolio was done, I got a meeting with the famed Wilhelmina Modeling Agency. I was told I had potential, but my lips were too full. Ha! Today, Angelina Jolie lips are all the rage.

So, there I was, having a total ball in New York. I continued learning fashion and was tempted by possible trips to Hong Kong and Paris during the latter part of those two years. There were parties, disco dancing, lots of dating . . . hmmm. Harvard Business School was never going to be *this* much fun. "Maybe I'm really not supposed to go," I thought. My patience to begin business school was starting to waver. "I can keep growing in the fashion business this way and start my own store here." I had it all planned out. I decided I was *not* going to go to Harvard after all and was going to tell my parents when I went home for Christmas.

When I got home to Detroit, my dad was sitting at the breakfast room table when I walked into the house. He looked up and when he saw me, beaming with pride, he said, "Here comes my Ivy League Baby! The first in our whole family!"

And that was that. I could not disappoint Dad. Having Patience snapped right back to the front of my mind. I had to continue to be patient about my own fashion store dreams. After the holidays, I went back to New York and finished my pre-calculus coursework and job responsibilities. When it was time, I packed up my Beetle and drove to Boston.

When I got to Harvard, there was real ivy on the walls—honest to God. That's the thing about Having Patience when you Pivot for Success. You often don't know you've made the right move until later on in the game.

Patience Is an Intermission Between Acts

In my first book, *Tap Into Your Juice*, I likened patience to intermission between acts in a play. The curtain comes down on Act 1 and the stage goes dark as things pause to get rearranged for Act 2. You have to wait for the curtain to rise again; in the meantime, a lot is happening that you can't see. In the same way, during the pause of patience as you Shift Your Energy, take some time to reflect and write down some positives you have learned along the way, at this stage or other parts of your life. By reflecting on what you've experienced thus far, you will see and feel the resilience you relied on before and draw upon that again as you move toward your goals. As

I reflect back on my life, despite having a take-charge personality and not wanting to wait for the things I want to happen, there are a number of experiences I've had where I realize Having Patience resulted in achieving my goals.

I wanted to be an entrepreneur from my youngest days making perfume from rose petals from my mother's garden and selling it in little bottles to her friends. What really gave me tremendous insight to being an entrepreneur was actually working for one of the best up close—Tom Burrell. Burrell Advertising was the largest ad agency in the country targeting African Americans. His clients included Coca-Cola, McDonald's, Ford Motor Company, Proctor & Gamble, and many other blue-chip companies. I met Tom in 1984 while I was working for the Gillette Company in New York City. We both happened to be at Jezebel's Restaurant in the Theater District at the same time. Tom was there with his team for dinner and I was there with some Gillette folks after a meeting for the Miss America pageant. Jezebel's was *the* spot to go to in New York at that time. Owned by Alberta Wright, it was the epitome of elegant soul food. The décor was as if you stepped into an antebellum home in the South, with beautiful shawls hanging from the ceiling, posters of Black films and Black art all around, chandeliers providing mood lighting—all enhanced by delicious aromas wafting from the kitchen. And the stars . . . I once saw Bruce Springsteen there, sitting on a porch swing hanging in the middle of the place with his then girlfriend, Patti. Miss Alberta was so gracious to me, letting me tour her kitchen when I told her of my other dreams of one day opening my own soul food restaurant. She told me, "Girl, it's a lot of hard work, but if your heart is in it, you should do it!"

I had followed Tom Burrell's work for years, given my love of advertising since Harvard Business School. His commercials for Coke and McDonald's were legendary. When I saw him in Jezebel's, I knew exactly who he was—tall, striking, debonair—and I walked right up to him and introduced myself, boldly saying, "Hello, Mr. Burrell. I love your work and one day I want to work for you." He laughed heartily, but then after I told him a bit about my background, he said, "Well, young lady, if you are serious, here's my card. Stay in touch." And that's what I did. Patiently, for almost two years, whenever I saw a new Burrell ad, I sent him a note of sincere congratulations. And in late 1985, Tom had me fly to Chicago to interview for an Account Supervisor's position. I got the job. I was super excited . . . but my husband was not. We were living in Boston, his engineering job was there, and things were shaky between us. He said, "Why don't you take the job; see if you like it. If you do, I'll join you then." Not great terms, but I was willing to take them. Chicago: Here I come! But . . . then I found out I was pregnant. And it had been hard to start a family. So, I had to turn Tom down, and Pivot my priorities to motherhood and Have Patience that another opportunity to work with Tom would surface.

By 1991, my husband had been accepted to go to Northwestern's Kellogg School of Business in Evanston, Illinois, a suburb of Chicago. He had followed me to Minneapolis several years earlier for a big Gillette promotion, so it was my turn to pivot and follow him to Chicago. Secretly, I was overjoyed. I had always wanted to live in Chicago. Coming from Detroit, Chi-Town was the big city. Moving to Chicago, I knew I needed a job, and the first person I reached out to was Tom Burrell. It was *six years* after his first job offer, but now he had an even bigger job in mind for me—SVP of Integrated Marketing of the new vision for his company, Burrell Communications. I had to write a proposal for that job; how I would integrate the three current divisions—Burrell Advertising, Burrell Promotions, and Burrell Public Relations—into one company, Burrell Communications. To get the job, I had to present my proposal to his board of directors. Well, I got it, and met other celebrated entrepreneurs on Tom's board who were helpful to me in future quests for a restaurant and other ventures. My patience had paid off. In those six years between job offers from Tom, I gained critically important experience that I ultimately brought to Burrell—senior experience at Gillette, the Pillsbury Company, and as a sales consultant with

Mary Kay Cosmetics, one of the first major cosmetic companies to understand the benefits of multicultural marketing. The Pivot of Having Patience between Act 1 way back in Boston and Act 2 in Chicago was tremendously positive. Even though at times it was stressful, I gained courage, strength, and optimism from the process. Patience breeds rewards almost every time.

My final example about Having Patience revolves around The ComfortCake Company, which I founded in 2001 based on my own pound cake recipes. We secured United Airlines as our first customer. Their purchase of 550,000 small slices gave us great credibility. I took that credibility and went to McDonald's in 2002, as they did not have a pound cake on their menu. I was summarily turned down. The company was focused on salads at the time. Year after year, I patiently and perseveringly (Pivot Point #9) went back. Finally, in 2009, a full *seven years* after my first attempt, we were able to gain a 50-store test market in the McDonald's system. This was unheard of for a product from a small supplier like my company. ComfortCake's Lemon Pound Cake performed well. But again, the menu focus for McDonald's changed. But patience and perseverance still got me in the door. My vision for The ComfortCake Company changed, too; we have pivoted to licensing the intellectual property of the business. I can share with you that my Having Patience is paying off in ways that I could not have imagined almost 20 years ago. I used the time of patience to revisit the vision for the company, shift the energy, and make moves toward our goals for sure.

The Importance of Having Patience

There's an old Chinese proverb: "One moment of patience may ward off great disaster, and one moment of impatience can ruin a life." Can you think of a time when you rushed into a decision that you wished you had thought about longer? Wisdom about what to do often comes when you are calm and detached from the urgency at hand in a situation. And often, it is hard to see clearly the best path ahead when your mind is cluttered with the dust of rushing thoughts pushing you to action too soon.

Here are the key lessons from Having Patience:

- Patience can be powerful; it can allow for the right time, the right situation, and the right resources to evolve and align.
- Patience provides unexpected lessons—waiting allows for intro-spection if you look for the meaning in the waiting.
- Patience can build confidence and courage as you look both inward and outward for direction and knowledge.
- The benefits of Patience are not always immediate—you will look back over time and be glad that you waited for what you wanted or needed—or thought you did.
- The Power of Patience can have both a calming and energizing effect on the people around you when, as a leader, you explain the benefits that Patience can bring.

7

Seeking Positivity

Positive thoughts and people are necessities, not luxuries.

MY DEAR FRIEND Susan Taylor and I first met when I was a sopho-more at Howard University, around 1972, and she had just become the Beauty Editor at *Essence* magazine. She came to campus looking for students to profile in the magazine. She was breathtakingly gor-geous, with a distinctive bald head at the time, wearing a glamorous outfit accessorized with bold jewelry. Of course, I came decked out in the best fabulousness I could afford at the time, thinking I would definitely be chosen to be profiled. I wasn't and was truly disap-pointed. But what I remember about meeting her was her gracious-ness as she met each student during the interviews. She made each of us feel beautiful.

Susan and I met again after I started working for Gillette in the 1980s, and by then she was Editor in Chief. *Essence* actually did profile me in 1983 as one of their "Women on the Move," and I was so gratified by that. Susan and I became friends over the years as I worked with *Essence* on several advertising campaigns in my different marketing roles. We talked about navigating life and how I learned so much from her speeches and books.

Several years ago, I was at a women's conference where Susan was the keynote speaker. When we talked after the conference, I told her about a challenge I was having with someone I considered difficult. Susan then shared this profound wisdom with me, and it has stayed with me since: *Everyone can't have a front-row seat in your life.* It was a revelation for me to recognize that I am not putting people out of my life necessarily, they are just not occupying ringside seats if they don't bring the positivity I need.

This perspective has been immensely helpful.

Choose Where People and Thoughts Sit in Your Life

When you Pivot for Success and Hone Your Vision, Shift Your Energy, and Make Your Move, there are many things pulling at you all at once. You may be evaluating significant areas of your life during a crisis and need a lifeline. Or you may finally be on the path toward the dream you have wanted for a long time. There is nothing worse than sharing your excitement or your major decision with someone important to you only to have them burst your bubble with silence, a negative comment, or indifference. Fighting negativity can feel like pushing a rock uphill. When making major life changes, managing your energy is imperative. There are only 24 hours in each day. You must choose how many of those precious hours you are going to spend trying to get others to be positive. Once you get a sense of where people are for you, make the choice which row they will sit in. It can be one of the hardest but most important choices you make.

You may ask: what if that person is a business colleague, family member, spouse, significant other, mentor, or close friend? This is when the skill of emotion management comes into play. Emotion management is not something to "get to later." It is an important life and business skill for success, and one that is worthy of mastering. Why? Let's start with business.

In recent years, there have been many articles and books published, and discussions held, on the value of Emotional Intelligence/Quotient (EQ) and how it is as important as IQ (Intelligence Quotient) in determining the potential for leadership success. I believe EQ is the ability to successfully regulate your emotions and understand the emotions of others for the most potentially positive outcome of a situation. IQ is more related to intellectual ability, such as the ability to learn quickly and well; it covers logic, word comprehension, and math skills. People with higher IQs are generally thought to be able to think better in the abstract and more easily make generalizations.

Until recent years, a high IQ was used as the measure of success professionally and in life. Now, however, some feel that a high IQ will get you through college, but a high EQ will get you through life. We often hear that people will do business with someone they like, even if the product or service from someone smarter is better. In a shift, many corporations now require their promising executives to take coaching on EQ skills, as they believe those with high EQ skills work better in teams, are self-starters, and manage others well. In addition, according to Seta Wicaksana, CEO of Humanika Consulting, people with high EQ skills:

1. Remain calm under pressure
2. Resolve conflict effectively
3. Are empathetic to their colleagues and act as such
4. Lead by example
5. Put more consideration into business decisions[1]

---

[1]Seta Wicaksana, "High EQ Skills," https://www.google.com/search?q=high+EQ+skills+-+Seta+Wicaksana&tbm=isch&ved=2ahUKEwj9uLy14_vuAhUJB50JHRiNApYQ2-cCegQIABAA&oq=high+EQ+skills+-+Seta+Wicaksana&gs_lcp=CgNpbWcQA1CylwpYss0KYP_WCmgAcAB4AIABVIgBwQKSAQE0mAEAoAEBqgELZ3dzLXdpei1pbWWfAAQE&sclient=img&ei=Jr0yYP2NCImO9PwPmJqKsAk&bih=789&biw=1440&hl=en#imgrc=1geV3BXiWLQPjM

As you can see in business, when Pivoting toward Seeking Positivity, emotion management skills are valuable to have. If you combine it with Pivot Point #2, Believing in Possibilities, there is something positive to learn in every situation, and Pivot Point #6, Having Patience, you can build the skill of emotion management into something powerful.

After Harvard Business School, I went back to Bloomingdale's. CEO Marvin Traub, an HBS grad himself and father of Andy Traub, who was my partner in an HBS real estate class project, personally and positively recruited me. It was hard to turn him down, even though I had a better salary offer and personal letter from Ed Ney, the chairman of Young and Rubicam Advertising, one of the legendary Madison Avenue ad agencies and, as related earlier, where I had done a summer internship while I was at Harvard.

So, once again, I was at Bloomingdale's. This time, I thought, for sure I'd be back in the fashion area of the store given my experience and MBA. Didn't happen. I was assigned to the Towel department. The Towel department! At first, I was very disappointed. There were not to be any "exploratory interviews" with another area of the store this time. I really had to Pivot to Seeking Positivity on that assignment. And guess what? It was there. Lesson: When you don't see Positivity in a situation immediately, give it some time. Importantly, assume it is there somewhere, even when you have to move the seats around in your life, *or in your mind,* to make it so.

What was positive about the Towel department? Quite simply, it was the most profitable department in the entire store. Who knew? I sure didn't. I often counsel people in business to follow the money. Learn where the money is and how the money is made. I learned a ton about business in general from being in the Towel department. Margins, supply chain, merchandising, vendor relationships, inventory control. Can I tell you I *hated* managing the staff to count 20,000 towels at inventory time? But I learned how to do it efficiently and effectively. The buyer, Norman Axelrod, was a brilliant merchant. Young, aggressive, with a high IQ and a high

EQ, he was amazing to work for. His staff loved working for him in New York and all the branches around the country. He was willing to teach me everything, but I had to move fast to keep up with him. And, together, in 1979, we produced the very first television commercials for Bloomingdale's! So, I did get to use my advertising and marketing skills after all. And it turned out it was so much fun and an awesome learning experience.

I was promoted from the Towel department in the New York store to run the Bath Shop and Towel departments at the Boston store, and then Women's Sportwear. While in Boston, I had the opportunity to work for a legendary merchant who I had always respected, who was the branch VP for Women's Clothing. She was "old school," spoke with a classic New York accent, could merchandise a floor in no time, and was feared by those who reported to her. I had a good relationship with her in New York when I worked at Bloomingdale's between Howard and Harvard Business School and was excited to learn from her in Boston. We got along well in the beginning, especially when my first big event—a fashion show held in my department—had excellent results. I had produced a catalog of the items in the show, which was placed on every seat so customers could check off what they wanted. After the show, they could go to the salespeople with their choices, and then right to the registers—a novel concept for moderate sportswear. My boss was impressed, although at first didn't believe it was my idea to do the catalog.

Later in the season, a huge shipment of 5,000 T-shirts came in from China. One entire wall of my department was wooden cubby holes for folded items such as T-shirts in summer and sweaters in the fall. The shipping department let me know those T-shirts were going to arrive on the selling floor at a certain time, and I knew I had to be prepared with my staff to get them into those cubby holes quickly by color and size so the cartons wouldn't be an eyesore. Armed with a pad of paper, pencil, shipping manifest, and a calculator, I started plotting out what would go where. Just then, my boss came on the selling floor and went totally ballistic. Talk about negativity! She yelled, "What do you think you are doing?? Get these T-shirts out of those cartons and into that wall *right now*!! You don't need a Harvard MBA to figure this stuff out." And she started throwing T-shirts into slots as my staff stood by dumbfounded.

Since she was my boss, I couldn't put her in a back-row seat in my life. But I could remove her from a front-row seat on the selling floor with my staff. I took a breath and calmly asked her if she would follow me into my office, and I started walking toward it, not waiting for an answer. Now my "office" was in the stockroom under the stairs. My staff had the good sense to clear out of there so it would just be the two of us. I was *seething* inside. But I looked my boss in the eye and *calmly* but *firmly* told her, "I have always respected you and wanted to work for you. I may report to you, but you do *not* have the right to speak to me that way, especially in front of my staff. If you have a problem with how I was preparing to merchandise the T-shirt wall, bring me back here to discuss it as professionals and teach me."

Emotion management led to a *big* Pivot to Seeking Positivity with respect, which is very important for all of us to establish. However, needless to say, we didn't have the best relationship after that. She was not used to being called out about her behavior, and let's just say her EQ was not high on the scale.

Lesson: When I was faced with a potentially combustible situation, I used a technique on that selling floor that I now know as STOP. I can't remember where or when I learned it, but it is *extremely* helpful in emotion management and can work in the moment. STOP stands for:

Stop

Take a Breath

Observe

Proceed

I highly recommend you recognize when you need to STOP and practice so you can pull it out when you need it.

After discussions with the head of the Boston store about the situation and my ultimate goal of moving into the marketing department of Bloomingdale's, I was finally told that a marketing career path would only happen after reaching the SVP level in merchandising. Well, Pivot Point #6, Having Patience, is important, but that would have taken several *years* to achieve, and I already had the marketing bug bad. Should I have taken the Y&R job instead of going back to Bloomie's right out of HBS? I've often thought about that over the years. But there was something about the client service aspect of account management versus the decision aspect of retail buying that pulled me—as well as the thought of someday being in marketing department for the great Bloomingdale's under the legendary Marvin Traub. In the end, I think Bloomingdale's was exactly where I needed to be at the time. But my long-term future was not there. I needed to Pivot to make my next move, Seeking Positivity.

Remember in Pivot Point #4, Envisioning Prosperity, how I spoke about the importance of building relationships? HBS is where I met Linda Keene, who became my mentor, friend, and later my boss. When I arrived at Harvard, she was a second-year student. Later, she worked at Gillette when I was at the Bloomindale's Boston store. Our relationship was a rarity—working for someone in executive ranks who was truly a close friend. Linda and I did it twice, at Gillette, then at Pillsbury. We kept in touch after HBS; Linda and her husband, Bob, introduced me to my husband. When I realized my dream of working, marketing at Bloomingdale's wasn't going to happen, I talked with Linda. I told her about Honing My Vision to get into marketing sooner rather than later. She told me that Gillette was looking for entry-level brand management people, and if I was willing to start at the bottom of the marketing ladder, I could probably get an interview. I used Pivot Point #2 and Believed in the Possibility that what happened negatively at

Bloomingdale's with my boss would lead me to something positive. Shifting My Energy, I used Pivot Point #5, Getting Prepared, did my research, got the interview, and, finally, the marketing job at Gillette that changed the trajectory of my professional career. In Pivoting to Seeking Positivity from a negative professional situation, even though I learned a tremendous amount and had many positive experiences at Bloomingdale's, I learned an invaluable lesson: *The momentum gained from moving toward that gives you positive energy is powerful on so many levels.*

Your Mind Can Move Mountains—One Way or the Other

On a personal level, Seeking Positivity is vital as well. Often when you are on a path that others just cannot visualize or understand, or is nontraditional, risky, or threatening to the status quo of the relationship you have, managing your emotions is again a vital skill. And it is a lifelong learning curve. There is a 90/10 Principle in life that, in my opinion, applies when dealing with negativity in others, particularly in those close to you or who? try to get close to you:

10% of life is what happens to you

90% of life is how you respond

Road rage is an example. Someone cuts you off on the highway. You can get angry and start a shouting match out your window that could dangerously escalate. Or, you could let the other driver have their way, and Shift Your Energy to a more positive thought—such as, you avoided an accident. With family members, significant others, and friends, it may be harder to actually move them from the row they may occupy in your life. When a big event happens in your life, you can choose *what* you share with them that could possibly trigger negativity toward your dreams and goals. In that way, what you are doing is moving their *negativity* to a back row. Take the time to become aware of the triggers and choose not to engage. Also choose how to respond when the feedback is not what you wanted, and instead choose to look inward for the fortitude to cheer yourself on or find others who you know will be there for you. It can be tough to move past the disappointment—I know, as I have been there. But that is why Pivot Point #7, Seeking Positivity, is under the second strategic process step of Shifting Your Energy. That is what is required. To Shift Your Energy toward positive aspects of the people close to you. They may come around as your endeavors move forward. They may not. Either way, you can choose how to respond.

The same is true about situations that when they are occur may be very negative. It is critical to Seek Positivity, especially when there is a situation of crisis.

My favorite cousin, Brett Denise Woodson, lived in Los Angeles. She'd come to visit me in Detroit, and as graduating high school seniors, our parents let us take a trip on our own to New York City in July. Coming from LA, she brought a wool coat with a fur-trimmed collar on the trip so she wouldn't get cold—in July! We had such a good time. She threw legendary New Year's Eve parties. When I went to HBS, she became a lawyer. We were in each other's weddings. And in 1988, she was killed when the Jeep Wrangler she was riding in during a vacation in Mexico went over a cliff.

Her parents were devastated, especially her father. My aunt, her mom, called and begged me to come and help with the funeral arrangements. I threw some clothes in a suitcase and immediately flew to LA. From the airport, my aunt took me to a wig store. Brett had beautiful long hair, and my aunt insisted on an open casket for the services. From the wig store, we drove directly to the funeral home—and went downstairs. There she was. I had to comb the wig on her head as the mortician put her face back together. It was an out-of-body experience.

I truly had to pray and think as hard as I could about something positive so I would not lose my mind. I kept silently asking Brett to "get up." As it became real to me that she would never be able to again, what came to me is this thought, *"As long as I can look up, I can get up."* I kept repeating that to myself over and over and over again. I repeated it all through the time I was in LA and said it aloud when I gave her eulogy. That phrase became seared into my soul.

As the years passed, whenever something negative happened to my children, friends, family, or when I'm speaking about overcoming challenges, I share that phrase. Not always the whole story of the devastating circumstance that it came from, but the power of Shifting Your Energy to move toward the positive. I shared it so often that unbeknownst to me, my son had it tattooed on his upper arm before he left home for college. It has certainly helped me keep things in perspective when I thought I had lost it all. When I stood that close to death and touched it, I *knew*: As long as I wasn't dead, I realized I could keep it moving.

Brett's sudden death when I was 36 was different from when my best friend was murdered in college when I was 19. Back then, I buried my feelings with work to maintain my sanity and graduate on time. With more maturity at 36 and beyond, I learned that in a crisis, it can help to take the time to recognize and stay aware of your feelings. By doing so, you can be in a better position to pivot toward the positive energy needed to make the best decisions and moves you possibly can. And even when those moves may not turn out like you wanted, by Seeking Positivity, you'll eventually see the lesson that was there for you to learn.

Surely, the vision I had when The ComfortCake Company was started was not the journey that has happened over the years. There were many heady years of terrific publicity and growing sales as I became known as "The Pound Cake Lady." I always had slices of ComfortCake in my business bag, as I never knew who I might come across in my travels. They were like business cards and I worked them like that! I am very proud of what The ComfortCake Company has meant to many people. Indeed, it has been a story of taking a recipe from my own kitchen and seeing the product on the shelves of Walmart, in the skies with United Airlines, and through the television screens of Home Shopping Network. The hard work that the ComfortCake team and I put in to make those successful milestones happen came with support from many fronts. I was fortunate to have learned from African American food entrepreneurs who took me under their wings, and my advisory board that helped me as I was navigating several tough decisions. They helped steer me toward Pivot Point #7, Seeking Positivity, when the light at the end of the tunnel was too weak to see.

Some of the hardest days were when dealing with bakery suppliers became challenging. We had to change bakeries a few times, and some changes worked better than others. The challenges included switching to cheaper ingredients, making more inventory than ordered, holding inventory from shipping, packaging incorrectly, charging more than they should, and more. During the recession of 2007–2008, these challenges were happening more regularly. Although not unusual in the food business, for a small business like mine that served large customers, such problems were not acceptable. I had to keep my mind on Seeking the Positive to negotiate toward solutions that were workable.

At times, however, when using Pivot Point #7, you must let people know you mean business and stand your ground. That is when Pivot Point #10, Managing Perceptions, comes into play. I did not want to leave the impression that I was a Pollyanna, just happy to take anything handed to me without complaint. Even as a small business, mutual respect must always be evident. Many people seem to think that the saying, "It's not personal, it's business," is true. I'm here to tell you, business is *personal.*

When negotiating from a Seeking Positivity mindset, yet going for the best business outcome, it is key to know what leverage you may have going in. In the case of my bakery suppliers, they wanted to be paid. If they did not adhere to the terms of my specifications, they wouldn't be.

Lesson: Always have clear specifications written out on orders, contracts, and other deliverables. That way, at the negotiating table, you can start from the positive, saying, "Here's what we agreed to. How can we both get what we need to be in agreement?"

When working with key suppliers, I can't impress more how important Seeking Positivity is. It works when there are challenges and when things are running smoothly. I have had relationships with some of my suppliers for almost 20 years. Most of them are used to working with much larger companies. My team and I were diligent in treating our supplier contacts with respect, geniality, and transparency. Establishing good relationships has been a touchstone for The ComfortCake Company and The Hilliard Group. In one case, one of the supplier contacts who was a sales manager when we first worked together is now the general manager of his entire company. The trust we have built with suppliers like these over the years has been invaluable, and we have been able to work through many tough business situations.

Another example of Seeking Positivity is meeting people face-to-face when possible. When I became president of Fashion Fair Cosmetics, one of the first things I did was to visit our cosmetic suppliers. I wanted to see who was making our products. While marketing has been my main expertise, manufacturing is also an area I understand. While I was visiting the main cosmetic supplier, the original chemist who developed the products for Mr. and Mrs. Johnson heard I was in the building. He came downstairs right away to meet me. He hadn't talked to anyone from the company in a long time. He was advanced in years, but extremely proud of the work he had done, and rightly so. I told him the product quality was excellent—as good as the major cosmetic brands were. He was so gratified. He told me, almost with tears in his eyes, "Miss Hilliard, that was what Mr. and Mrs. Johnson wanted for Black women, and I was proud to be able to make products that way for them." I never forgot that conversation. I was able to tell it to audiences of women in order to re-engage them with the Fashion Fair brand, and it made a difference to them.

Lesson: There are people behind products. Seeking Positivity can be a powerful way to let people know you care about the talent they bring to the work they do for you.

An additional way Seeking Positivity works is when you need to present material that can be hard for your audience to accept or absorb. This was the challenge for many years for The Hilliard Group. In the early to mid-1990s, major corporations were wrestling with the data presented from the 1990 US Census, which for the first time charted that 25% of the US population was people of color. And the predictions were that the percentage of people of color in the United States would continue to grow significantly. Think about it. Look where we are today in terms of the percentages of people of color in the United States and the discussions that abound regarding diversity. Back then, this was groundbreaking and, in some cases, scary news to executives. It is still challenging to discuss today.

Learning from the success of the *"Savor the Cultural Flavor"* seminar I created for The Pillsbury Company that gave executives a tasty way to understand how diverse populations used Pillsbury products, I developed a presentation to open minds about the changing face of America. It was called:

THE TEN COMMANDMENTS OF DIVERSITY MARKETING
Follow These Ten Commandments and You Will Be Able to Part the Red Ink Sea

Commandment #1 was:
SEEK DIVERSITY AND YE SHALL FIND MONEY
Don't Count the Numbers You Reach, Reach the Numbers Who Count

Using that format for the other nine Commandments with data and cultural insights, but not in a heavy-handed way, I was able to get corporations across America to think differently about multicultural marketing, always tying it to a strategic business imperative. Corporations from American Express to HBO to Ford Motor Company brought me in to speak to their teams, and we were able to have effective business-building discussions.

As you pursue your path, you will encounter positive and negative experiences. But by Seeking Positivity, you can turn it all into positives that teach and shape you, guide your path, and help you make your next move.

P↕VOT

Seeking Positivity Is More Powerful Than You Might Think

Like Having Patience, pivoting to Seeking Positivity has impact beyond measure—not just in business but in life. It opens up pathways that negativity can keep closed. Like all the Pivot Points, Seeking Positivity is a mindset that is flexible for the situations at hand, and is most effective when you to let it become part of you so that it is there when you need it.

Here are the key lessons from Seeking Positivity:

- Everyone can't have a front-row seat in your life.
- Emotion Management and Emotional Quotient abilities are critical skills to learn.
- If you don't see Positivity immediately, give it some time or try a different way.
- Remember the 90/10 Principle—How you respond in life matters most. The STOP technique can help, too.
- You can Seek Positivity and still hold your ground.
- The momentum of Positivity is powerful on many levels.

Part III: Make Your Move

8

Honoring Your Passion

It's the lubricant that keeps your dreams alive.

WHAT WERE YOUR childhood dreams? How many of us have forgotten our childhood dreams of becoming a ballerina, astronaut, or doctor? There may be other unfulfilled aspirations that are still haunting you like the melody of a favorite song. Maybe you dreamed of making a million dollars, writing a best-selling novel, starting a restaurant, or designing a car. At some point in your life, you had passionate energy around those goals.

Think about it: By the time most people finish college, they will have spent over 20,000 hours in school. How many of those hours did you spend thinking about what makes you excited to pursue? Finding what you are passionate about and incorporating that into your life can give you success, sanity, and spiritual fulfillment. This Pivot Point is about giving yourself permission to pursue what you long to do by listening to your instincts and stepping out on faith to do what you were meant to do. I consider Honoring Your

Passion to be the lubricant for your dreams, because it can fuel all the other Pivots you need for success. It can drive your commitment to Finding Your Purpose, Believing in Possibilities, and Defining Your Priorities. Passion inspires you to Get Prepared, instills the power of Having Patience, keeps you Seeking Positivity, awakens the stamina to Maintain Perseverance, and underlines the importance of Managing Perceptions.

But here's the thing. Passion is like oil in a car. A car won't run without it, but a car can't run on oil alone. Far too often, people rely on passion to make their dreams happen, and when they don't materialize, they wonder why. People can fall passionately in love with the *idea* of success. For this reason, I say that Passion without a plan can end up being a lot of hot air. You still have to do the work and build the foundation that will Honor Your Passion into reality.

Passions Can Evolve and Stand Strong with Effort

We all can't be Pablo Picasso, who knew at a young age he was destined to be an artist, and that was all he wanted to do. For others, passions evolve, grow, and change. I've had several passions: ballerina, actress, fashion store owner, retail fashion buyer, model, restaurant owner, brand marketer, family woman, multicultural marketer, marketing consultant, food entrepreneur, speaker, and health advocate. I've been fortunate to have been able to try my hand at each of these passions in enough depth to decide what worked best for me at the stage of life I was in.

That's the thing about Pivoting to Honor Your Passion. You can have more than one passion and honor each of them, but it needs to be done with enough depth so that you aren't just flitting from one thing to the next. My list of passions is many years long—from my preteen years to now in my 60s. So, I've had the time to explore. It may seem to others that you are flitting from one passion or one idea to another, and that can be frustrating to those close to you who may be more comfortable with a straighter path. At the same time, I believe it takes courage to move your life toward your passions, and the same courage to know when to act on them.

Ask your head, your heart, and your soul what moves you. Each of these areas can provide balance to your passions and helps to make them actionable. When you ask your head, you can look back on the Pivot of Defining Your Priorities for indications of critical things to consider. But put those aside for a moment. Now look at your heart and soul. Go back and consider the Pivots of Finding Your Purpose and Believing in Possibilities. Your passions are there—how do you *feel* about your Purpose and Possibilities? What is giving you energy in spite of the practical work it will take to accomplish what you need to bring your dreams to life? This is what you are passionate about. It could be the whole dream itself, or the part that it takes to make the dream happen. Stay open to the options that present themselves. Let me share a story about staying open to those options.

Like many women, I've changed my hairstyle a lot. Long, short, straight, curly, natural. I've had a lot of people who have worked on my hair and I have gotten to know them and their specialties. When I decided recently to go back to wearing my hair very short and curly, I returned to the barber I started with over 15 years ago. Zarif has been with the same barbershop in Chicago for a long time. On a recent visit, we started talking about how he decided to become a barber. I asked him if it was his passion because it's such a precise skill. He said, no, not originally. His first passion, as young boy, was to become a policeman. Then he became interested in martial arts. He always liked to draw and was creative as well. As he became older, to bring money into his household, he saw how lucrative being a cosmetologist could be. He started styling women's hair and was very good at it. Seeking a better opportunity, Zarif applied to a "hair salon" ad in a local paper. The salon turned out to be a barber shop that also had some female clientele. The owner tried him out, and Zarif did so well that he was hired on the spot. Soon, even though he had not trained to be a barber, Zarif started working on male customers, who liked his results. Competitive by nature and disciplined from his martial arts training, he watched the other barbers and learned his craft very well. He *became* passionate about being a barber and built up a steady clientele. Soon, a young man came in and became a regular customer of Zarif's. They got along wonderfully, talking about the neighborhood, politics, and changing the world. That young man was Barack Obama. Zarif has been Barack Obama's barber since before he was in politics and through both his terms as president of the United States.

Lesson: Sometimes, you can't plan your passion. Fulfilling a priority in your life may turn it into a passion and there's no telling where it may take you!

Another lesson I've learned about Honoring Your Passion is how important it is to test your passion to see if it's something you really want to build a project, business, or your life around.

As mentioned in Having Patience, in 1992, I had to present to Tom Burrell's Board of Directors to get the job of SVP at his firm. Larry Levy of Levy Restaurants was on the board. After meeting him, I mentioned to Larry that one day I hoped to have my own restaurant. He chuckled, but said if I was serious, to let him know and he'd be happy to talk with me about it. Levy Restaurants started in 1978 with a delicatessen in Chicago's Water Tower Place. His company is now a giant in the hospitality industry, with over 200 sports and entertainment venues in 41 markets throughout the United States and Canada, and also owns and operates several restaurants. In 2004, the company revenue was over $470 million, and by 2017 it had grown to over $1.5 billion.

I had harbored the passion of owning a restaurant for many years in different cities where I lived—Boston, Minneapolis, and Chicago. I had written business plans, and seriously looked at leasing space. However, I had never actually worked in one. After starting The Hilliard Group, I reconnected with Larry in 1995 and he graciously offered me the chance to shadow the general manager of one of his popular restaurants on the Gold Coast of Chicago. The restaurant was about the size of the one I was considering opening. There was a space in an up-and-coming area of Chicago and if I could raise the right capital, I could start an upscale soul food restaurant—there was not one in the city at that time. Larry understood the opportunity but felt that working in a restaurant would really test my passion, and I agreed. He was right.

The general manager of the restaurant was excellent, showing me the inner workings of how to successfully run an operation. I enjoyed it. The pace was energizing. As the owner, I would have to know the front of the house, the back of the house (kitchen operations), purchasing, staffing. Sure, I had all of this in my business plan. However, seeing it in action was a whole other dimension. I had to step back and assess whether Pivoting to Honor my Passion for a restaurant would be in alignment with how I was Defining My Priorities of my family. The hours would be grueling, even though I wouldn't be traveling. And truth be told, I am not an operations person. And that is what you really need to be to run a restaurant, in my opinion. That has to be your passion. Making sure the trains are running on time. All of them.

I am so grateful to Larry Levy for that experience in his restaurant. We still chuckle about it whenever we run into each other. Again, my passion for working for Burrell led me to delve more into my passion about owning a restaurant. Working for a restaurant taught me a lot about the food business that was invaluable when I formed The ComfortCake Company, but also taught me that owning a restaurant was not for me.

Lesson: Honoring Your Passion can be a road map that, if you follow and test it, can give you the experience you need for the passion that will be your sustaining one—or help you weed out passions that ultimately aren't right for you.

Be Patient with Your Passion

This leads me to another facet of Honoring Your Passion: seeing your passion come to fruition takes time. You must be committed to diving deep enough into your passion to see if it is for you, and test it, but also stick with it long enough to give it time to materialize. Farmers who plant seeds and then pick the fruit before it ripens will not reap the full rewards of their work. How do you know when to hold 'em and when to fold 'em? There are times when holding on too long to a dream can be detrimental to your finances, job prospects, and key priorities. There is no template to use for this decision, and this can be scary. However, it can be the time to keep moving through your fear. I think of fear as **F**aith **E**ventually **A**ttracting **R**esources.

Debbie Allen, the multitalented actor/producer, is an example of this. She was the producer of the award-winning 1997 film *Amistad* directed by Steven Spielberg. The movie was based on the true story of the events in 1839 aboard the slave ship *La Amistad* where the Mende tribesmen of Africa who had been abducted for the slave trade gained control of the ship off the coast of Cuba. The legal battle that ensued was ultimately resolved by the US Supreme Court in 1841.

When Debbie told me that it took her *18 years* to get this movie done, I was awestruck. I asked her what kept her going. "My passion to tell this story, and faith that it would happen," was her answer. "It kept leading me to the right people to help. When I was able to get a meeting with Steven Spielberg and he got engaged after so many people said 'no,' I knew we would get it done." The film, starring Anthony Hopkins, Morgan Freeman, Matthew McConaughey, and Djimon Hounsou, and with a music score by John Williams, won Oscars, Golden Globes, Grammys, and other prestigious awards. When I saw it at a premier screening in Chicago, I had no idea how long it took to bring it to life until Debbie told me in 2019. To Pivot to Honoring Your Passion takes Having Patience and Believing in Possibilities along with all of the other Pivot Points.

Like Debbie Allen, when people Pivot to Honoring their Passions, they often speak of having faith that the things they are passionate about will come to pass. I believe this as well. In fact, I believe that a foundation of faith is vital for this Pivot Point, and the Pivot of Believing in Possibilities. To put my belief about faith and success succinctly it is: *if you are spiritually connected, you will be economically directed.* I created an acronym to use the word faith as an action word:

F—*Focus* in on what you want

A—*Accept* your Greatness and **Assume** Success

I—*Intuitively* use **Insight** and

T—*Trust* in the process to find

H—*Harmony* in Life

As the **F** indicates, focus is important. Yet, Debbie Allen has multiple passions, as do I, and you probably do, too. Depending on your personality, risk profile, energy level, and abilities, you can work successfully at more than one passion at a time. What may seem like multiple passions may actually be passions that are within common themes, which can provide synergy for your energy. Debbie Allen is a *performing artist* in film, stage, and television. Larry Levy is in the *hospitality industry* with sports, entertainment venues, and restaurants. I am a *marketer and entrepreneur* in the hair care, cosmetics, and food categories with a *multicultural specialty* that resonates across several consumer purchasing categories of business. When looked at that way, it is not so scattered after all. The lesson here is that if you have multiple passions, you can more easily Pivot to honor them if they have synergy.

As the stages of your life evolve, Honoring Your Passion can be reignited. For example, you may have been passionate about painting when you were younger, but Defining Your Priorities pulled you away from your art as you raised your family. Look at Grandma

Moses. She started painting professionally at 78 years old and one of her paintings sold for $1.2 million in 2006. It's never too late. What can help to reignite your passion is to prune away the things that no longer serve you. Pruning helps you Honor Your Passion by making room in your life for you to Pivot toward what gives you joy, purpose, and possibilities. As you Hone Your Vision, you can evaluate how you may now want to live your life: whether that's more simply, in a warmer climate, or with fewer possessions. Shifting Your Energy to get rid of excess things and downsize into what really fits you can be an amazing step to free your mind and help you Make Your Move toward passions you forgot you had!

When I moved from my large condo a few years ago, I came across my old modeling portfolio that I created after college when I lived in New York before going to Harvard Business School. I was truly passionate about becoming a model. Many people had told me I had the look for it, and having seen professional models in my fashion work, I thought, why not me? Looking through those pictures and realizing that in today's marketplace there is an interest in the Baby Boomer demographic, I created a blog called *Sizzling After 60—How to Thrive at Every Stage of Your Life*. It features pictures of me doing fun things, modeling some trendy outfits, and sharing healthy living tips. I post when I can, and it is a passion I will continue to build on. In 2020, my blog was named one of the best blogs for women over 50, and who knows, my modeling career may yet take off!

Importantly, Shifting My Energy to Make the Move and leave the condo was timely. Pruning to get rid of clothes, furniture, books, artifacts, files, dishes, and more was the pruning I needed to give my life fresh air to Pivot to Honor my Passion of writing this book, something I've wanted to do for at least 15 years. When you release the unnecessary weight of possessions, and in Seeking Positivity move the right people and thoughts into your life, it makes room for your passions to come back to life or be (re)discovered.

Pruning to Seek Positivity to Honor Your Passion is so important that I must stop here for a moment. When you have the energy of people in your orbit who get your vision, it is a scientific reality—physics, really—that creates the momentum that similar energies can create. Passion is infectious. It is so powerful. Everyone wants to be around it. It can build companies, corporations, communities, families. Yet it must be authentic. Don't fake the funk. Folks can tell. Stand for what you believe. You'll find a tribe that does, too. That is Honoring Your Passion. To Pivot toward action with Honoring Your Passion, start with the energy around you and realize it is a process of building a foundation on top of the excitement you feel about something for it to last.

Honoring Your Passion does not mean you will do things that impact the world on a seismic level. This is what I think stops people from stepping out there. Not everyone is Albert Einstein or George Washington Carver. Do *you*. Your fingerprint is valid and unique. Each one can teach one. I remember my first-grade teacher, Mrs. McFadden, well. She was so kind, yet quite strict about teaching us how to write. Handwriting was something she took seriously. Curating each letter was how she approached her task with us, making each letter important in its own right. It was her passion and I loved it. To this day, I do not understand how someone can sign something with a signature that no one can read legibly. I am proud of mine, and it is because Mrs. McFadden Honored Her Passion.

Your passion can also evolve from addressing an issue that has bothered you for a while. You may not be passionate about the company or industry where you work currently, but you can be passionate about correcting an issue within an industry and see an opportunity to do better. This can certainly turn into a passion if you keep your options open. Richard Branson of Virgin Airways certainly felt this way about banking services. Studying the passions of others can be instructive.

Richard Branson is an innovative entrepreneur, known most for Virgin Airways. He has had several spin-offs, including Virgin Money in 1995, which was developed to make banking easier and more accessible for people. He wasn't particularly interested in banking but has a passion for customer service. In fact, it is the core of everything Virgin stands for. His philosophy about passion is, "If you have an idea that might work in an area that you're not passionate about, instead think about ways that you could apply it to a sector that does excite you. Look at your idea from a different perspective, and you might be surprised by the results."[1] Branson further says, "When you have an 'aha!' idea, pay attention: Perhaps that idea will help you to identify a market gap, or even to disrupt an industry."

Branson also believes in passion as a lubricant, as I do. "When you believe in something the force of your convictions will spark other people's interest and motivate them to help you achieve your goals. This is essential to success."

This is exactly what happened in my marketing career at Gillette. I loved brand marketing, creating and recreating new products like White Rain Shampoo. However, I saw a market gap: Gillette wasn't promoting their products to African Americans. I *became* passionate about addressing that gap and disrupting Gillette's approach to marketing. Others became motivated about the opportunity and in the process, my career took off in ways in ways I never imagined.

I believe Honoring Your Passion does something else: it develops mastery. It turns you toward doing what you are intrinsically good at. Donald O. Clifton, chairman of the Gallup Organization, wrote a best seller called *Soar with Your Strengths* some years ago. It's one of my favorite books. In it he recommends people to study harder at what they are already good at instead of trying to get better at their weaker subjects. When you study what you are already good at, you can become great at it. Once I discovered my passion, I spent many years studying the platform of multicultural marketing that was within the broader marketing sphere. I became known for

[1]Natalie Clarkson, "Richard Branson: The Importance of Passion in Business" (March 24, 2015), Virgin website, https://www.virgin.com/about-virgin/latest/richard-branson-importance-passion-in-business

it and have used this passion to create strategic business opportunities for corporations and important visibility for consumers of color.

Can you also see the intersection of Honoring My Passion and Finding My Purpose? To get corporations to understand the strategic business opportunity in marketing to people of color (my passion) I had to inspire them (my purpose). This is an example of how the 10 Pivot Points work together so well. They intersect with flexibility to cross check that you are on the right path for your best life.

In the building years of The ComfortCake Company, I can look back and see how Honoring My Passion fueled the momentum of the business. Not only did it secure United Airlines as our first customer, but it was important in most of the key aspects of getting the company off the ground. To create our logos and packaging, I had to convince large suppliers to take me on as a customer, making them believe that one day our volume would be worth their while. In the summer of 2001, I went to the Fancy Food Show in Chicago to become more knowledgeable with the industry I was getting into. I visited the booths of competitors and potential suppliers as I walked the trade show floor. At one booth, I met the general manager of one of the premier printing companies in the business, who printed packaging for many of the major food companies in the specialty food industry. Their work was exceptional, and I passionately told him our start-up story. He agreed to take on our business. I flew to their plant in Tulsa, Oklahoma, and was greeted with a "Welcome ComfortCake Company" sign. After a tour of the impressive and huge plant, I will never forget watching as the first print run for our signature red boxes came off the presses. I stood next to a big, burly print guy with a beard and wearing a red bandana, and a giant new $3 million printing press from Germany that he was very proud to operate. We had been talking, and as he was setting up the run I passionately shared with him how I started The Comfort-Cake Company. He got excited about our company, and of course, I brought samples for him and the other printing team members to taste. When the run started, I *felt* his dedication to making sure everything was perfect for me and my little company. It brought tears to my eyes.

Lesson: The contagiousness of passion is real and can make a huge difference in making dreams come true.

As the ComfortCake business started to grow, I was asked to speak at several of the Fancy Food shows across the country: New York, San Francisco, and Chicago. I was dedicated to sharing with others how we got started and what it meant to be part of the specialty food industry. My passion for the business got me noticed by the leaders in the industry, and I was asked to run for a seat on the board of directors for the National Association of the Specialty Food Trade. I ran and became the first African American elected to their board. It was a wonderful experience and was helpful to my business in many ways. And it came to pass all because I Honored My Passion.

The same thing happened with The Hilliard Group. One of my clients was Aetna Health Care. I was making a big presentation to their key executives on multicultural marketing, and Earl Graves Sr., the founder of *Black Enterprise* magazine, was in attendance. Although we had met in the past, I did not know he was going to be there. I passionately presented "The Ten Commandments of Diversity Marketing" at that meeting. Afterward, Earl came over to me and said that he wanted to nominate me to be on the PepsiCo Multicultural Advisory Board, which was in the process of forming. I was truly humbled and honored to serve and did so for 13 years, working closely with three PepsiCo CEOs. It is amazing the places that Honoring Your Passion can lead you to.

My sisters are also examples of Honoring their Passions. Pamela Hilliard Owens turned her passion for writing into a global consulting business. Gloria Mayfield Banks's passion for inspiring women to lead extraordinary lives led her to becoming the #1 National Elite Sales Director at Mary Kay Cosmetics. My sister Wendy Hilliard, a former international rhythmic gymnast and member of the Gymnastics

Hall of Fame, has turned her passion for gymnastics into the Wendy Hilliard Foundation, where she has trained over 20,000 underprivileged youth in the sport.

It is amazing the places that Honoring Your Passion can lead you to, and many benefits can be gained from it in business and in every aspect of your life. As you Hone Your Vision, Shift Your Energy, and prepare to Make Your Move, let Honoring Your Passion fuel the way.

The Power of Passion

From deep experience, I totally believe that passion is the lubricant that can keep your dreams alive. When I've had obstacles in front of me, fatigue on my shoulders, competitors on my back, and no one cheering me on, my passion created the energy to keep me going and motivated those I needed to help me, and it can for you, too. Trust me—after you've presented your business plan 50 times, passion will kick in for the 51st time when the investor who is ready for you happens to be in the room. Passion can't work alone, but it is what works with the other key Pivot Points to create the foundation for your dreams to stand on. Honor it.

Here are the key lessons from Honoring Your Passion:

- Passion shifts your energy, which makes you more attractive to investors and stakeholders.
- When you honor your passion, you create a road map that keeps you ahead of your competitors and in the game.
- Prune your life to what brings value and positivity, so your passion has room to flow.

- Passion makes work feel less like work, and while it takes time, inspires you to master your passion.
- Passion gives you something in common with other like-minded people.
- Passion engages others toward your vision when leading, teaching, and selling.

9

Maintaining Perseverance

Developing "bounce-backability" is imperative.

DETERMINATION. STICK-TO-ITIVENESS. NEVER, *never, never give up.*
We've all heard such words of encouragement a lot. Sir Winston
Churchill was known for them, encouraging the British people in
the depths of World War II. It is said that such resolve helped the
British endure and emerge triumphant from the war.

This mindset of Perseverance is one that you must have and
maintain to Pivot for Success. The reason is simple: things rarely go
exactly as planned. Shift happens—and that is not a typo. Things
shift. Murphy's Law kicks in. The competition beats you to the end
zone. A pandemic hits the world, and suddenly your own world
changes in ways you never imagined—how you work, how you live,
with whom you interact and how.

As you Pivot toward success, unforeseen events will arise.
How you respond will determine if you eventually get there. In my
life, I have relied on the Serenity Prayer to help me when I face

uncertainty and challenges. Indeed, it has helped millions respond in times of upheaval:

> God, grant me the serenity to accept the things I cannot change, the courage to change the things I can, and the wisdom to know the difference.

When you break these phrases down in challenging situations, it can bring much-needed calm to your mind, as well as courage to your heart and fortitude to empower your decision-making process. It has for me, many times.

On a lighter note, I also keep the Energizer Bunny in mind. That little critter keeps going and going and going no matter who or what tries to stop him. It keeps its batteries charged up and ready to go. And that's exactly what you have to do to Pivot to Maintaining Perseverance.

Bounce-backability: The Harder the Fall, the Higher the Rise

Throughout this book, I have shared some stories of challenges I've faced in my career and life and hinted that I've used this Pivot Point to overcome them. Every time I persevered, I developed "bounce-backability." This concept came to me as I watched my kids play in our backyard with rubber balls left over from my racquetball days. They loved to throw them down as hard as they could to see whose ball would bounce back up the highest. In watching them one afternoon, I saw clearly that the harder the balls were thrown down, the higher they bounced back. And that's how it has been with the challenges I've faced.

I experienced some setbacks in The ComfortCake Company about 2003 when I was going into and expanding retail distribution. After first selling our Bundt cakes at a small local grocery store with good results, we were able to get space selling them in 25 Jewel Food stores, the largest retail food chain in Chicago. At first, sales did very well. Then, the trend toward lower-carb eating became all the rage. People started decreasing their purchases of larger sizes of sweet baked goods. The buyer of baked goods called me and said, "Amy, your cakes are not doing well anymore. We are going to have to discontinue them." At this point, I actually utilized a twist on the Serenity Prayer that activist Angela Davis has been known to say much more recently:

I'm no longer accepting the things I cannot change . . .
I'm changing the things I cannot accept.

—*Angela Davis*

I didn't have those exact words in mind at the time, but I understood the concept. I was *not* going to accept that we were going to be discontinued at Jewel. No way, no how. I was going to Pivot and Maintain Perseverance. I used my time-tested technique of keeping the door open and asked for an "exploratory meeting" to see what the buyer needed more of in his department, given the changing trends in low-carb eating. At the meeting, I let him know that I put the needs of his department and the consumers first. We talked through what he saw consumers wanting and buying. It was about portion control. Consumers still wanted sweets, just not big portions of them in the house.

It was vital to change the perspective of the issue, and also use Seeking Positivity to do so. He asked me, "Amy, can you make ComfortCake in individually wrapped slices?" As it just so happened, I was in discussions about moving production to another bakery as I wasn't happy about the quality consistency at the bakery that had taken over after our first large contract production facility went out of business. The new bakery I was considering I found through relationships forged as I was attempting to sell to McDonald's. I met Bob Beavers, one of the key African American bun suppliers to McDonald's, through Patricia Harris, then McDonald's Chief Diversity Officer. He recommended a bakery that made a lot of pound cake and *specialized* in individually wrapped slices. Producing individually wrapped slices was no small endeavor, as major equipment was required as well as storage capacity. We had only just started initial talks that were positive, but based on Bob's recommendations, I felt confident we could get ComfortCake slices made. So, I told the Jewel buyer we could do it and asked for a test in a few stores. He agreed! We kept the business from being discontinued long enough to prove we were worth keeping in the stores we had in distribution.

Within a few weeks—and I mean just a few weeks—we had ComfortCake Lemon slices in basic displays with rather generic labels, but our ComfortCake red and white logos stood out strong. And they *sold out*! We got a reorder and started working on new upgraded graphics—colorful and impactful—for our slices in all our flavors. Those sold out as well. We expanded to over 100 stores, and the buyer soon started advertising ComfortCake slices weekly in the Jewel mailer that went throughout the city. Talk about bounce-backability! That ball bounced back up high. We were on a roll.

An important lesson about bounce-backability, however, is that you can't keep all your balls in the air at the same time. Sometimes a ball has to drop when it doesn't add value to a customer or situation at hand. We found this to be true as the Bundt cakes at Jewel were still slow sellers. We had to make the decision to ease out of those items and move them to e-commerce distribution exclusively, customer by customer. We had them with other retailers and had to move cautiously so as to not to take returns, which would have hurt our bottom line.

Maintaining Perseverance: Protecting What You Create

As I mentioned back in Pivot Point #4, Envisioning Prosperity, in Thanksgiving 2002, I had been making my usual ComfortCakes for the many family members in from all over the country. My dad was enjoying the ComfortCakes a *lot*. I'd come downstairs and there he'd be, coffee in hand, and crumbs on his face with a Cheshire Cat grin saying, "Good morning, honey!" And I kept telling him, "Daddy! You cannot keep eating so much ComfortCake! You are diabetic and there's too much sugar in it!" He looked at me and gave me my marching orders to make a ComfortCake he could eat that tasted as good as the original.

When I got back to my office, I contacted a friend who knew the CEO of Merisant, the parent company of the sugar substitute Equal. I was able to gain his approval to work with the Equal R&D team to try and make a sugarless ComfortCake. The R&D team was excited, and the marketing team said if it worked, they would be happy to put the Equal logo on our red boxes. We tried for six months. In doing so, we found out some important information: most sugar substitutes do not have all the baking properties of sugar. Sugar sweetens, bakes at high temperatures, browns, and bulks for density. To get any sugar substitute to do all four of those things, our commercial recipe had to be completely changed. Unfortunately, the texture was not what I wanted nor what our customers were used to. Back to the drawing board.

At the advice of my advisory board, I hired a food scientist to make me a sugarless pound cake recipe. I explained that I did not want to change the commercial recipe that had taken a year to complete. Just take out the sugar and add some of "this stuff" so that the cake was sugarless. She said there was no such thing, and I said, fine. That is what I need you to do with me. So, for 18 months, that is what we did. I worked with her: tasting, making suggestions for, and approving every single batch of product until we had what is now called Sugarless Sweetness. It is a cup-for-cup, granulated sugar substitute with no aftertaste—and it has been hailed as a break-through by many professional bakers. It can also be used in other food applications.

Just as we were going into production, we were contacted by the Food Network, which wanted to do a story on ComfortCake. We had been fortunate to have gotten a fair amount of publicity, and I was humbled to have been contacted by them. We agreed for them to film us baking our Sugarless Sweetness ComfortCake at the bakery. I had moved all Bundt production produced for the Chicago Public Schools (CPS) business to the bakery, as we were selling them Bundt cakes at that time. The Sugarless Sweetness Comfort-Cakes would be sold only on our website after being promoted on the Food Network. After the first showing, we *sold out* of them all over the country! Then, our other cakes on our website started selling as well. So, as we were moving our Bundt cakes out of retail distribution, our e-commerce distribution of them bounced back mightily. For over a year afterward, we would see upticks on the sales of Sugarless ComfortCakes on the website, and sure enough, it was because our Food Network episode was repeated.

I was so very proud of the extension of the product line from the ComfortCake business into ingredients with Sugarless Sweetness. However, it took an extreme Pivot of Maintaining Perseverance. You see, when I contracted to work with the food scientist, it was originally for a sugarless pound cake *recipe*, not an ingredient. So, the fee I paid when I contracted for the recipe to be developed had to be renegotiated for the development of an ingredient. It took me *seven years* to pay for it. I was and still am determined not to allow anyone to own something I conceived of, directed the creation of, and paid for unless it is monetized for the value that has been created. It has cost me a *lot* of money to protect and retain the intellectual property.

Lesson: Steadfastly protect what you create, so you can gain the value of it in the future.

Knowing the value of what you bring to the table is a key part of the Pivot of Maintaining Perseverance. It can mean holding out for the right pricing or contract under tense negotiations. This is when you must not only Maintain Perseverance, but also Believe in Possibilities so you don't fall into scarcity thinking. This is what happened one year with our biggest customer, the Chicago Public Schools. We had started with CPS about 2003, selling them our

Lemon Bundt cakes, which they then sliced into small portions to give to the children with their lunches. While the children loved them, it was an inefficient process for the lunchroom staffs to handle. We were asked if we could make presliced loaves with small slices that would come in frozen, so they could be thawed, and plated on the children's trays. In addition, to comply with new regulations, we needed to change our recipe to be trans-fat free. We worked with our bakery to come up with that solution and providing presliced loaves, and it worked for several semesters. Then CPS moved to a program of baking desserts right in the schools. They asked us what we could provide so they could efficiently do that with Comfort-Cake. We worked with our bakery to come up with a ComfortCake batter that could be frozen and shipped. It was easy for the CPS cafeterias to work with: just thaw, pour into a sheet cake pan, bake, slice, and serve. We were willing to accept what product changes they needed and to change our process to maintain the relationship.

The Courage to Accept and to Change

We had good relations with CPS and worked hard to meet their needs, even going beyond product improvements. I spoke often at schools as a role model for the students, so they could see there was a real person behind the ComfortCake brand. My hope was that many would be inspired to consider entrepreneurship in their future. However, with each product improvement made for CPS, we had to make cost adjustments to hold their pricing, which affected our profits. Our volume held for the most part. However, after the move to frozen batter, when it was time to negotiate our contract for the next year, I anticipated an increase in volume due to the major reduction in labor costs on their end and the increase in the number of servings we were told would be added to the menus the next year. Imagine my surprise when I was called into the purchasing manager's office to sign our contract and read that the volume was the same as the year before. I calmly asked, "Please help me understand why our business is not being increased. We have done everything that has been asked of us to build more efficiency into the production process for CPS and reduced your labor costs. In return, an increase in volume was indicated, given the number of servings that can now be produced."

The purchasing manager pushed his other papers aside, looked up at me and blithely said, "Hmm, yes. ComfortCake. I think we've given you enough business." I couldn't believe what I'd just heard, but kept a poker face and said to him, "Just so I'm clear, is that what you would say to Sara Lee? To Hostess Twinkies? To Betty Crocker? I don't think so. I am not signing this contract until this can be discussed further."

He got quite animated and said, "You have to sign today, or you won't have a contract." And so, as I got up to leave, I said to him, "Then I won't have a contract today. But I will have a contract. Thanks for your time."

I had to have to *courage* to accept the things I couldn't change, which was signing the contract that day, and the *courage* to change the things I could not accept, which was no increase in volume. That was an unacceptable situation given all the work we had done to earn it. To Pivot and Maintain Perseverance, I had to have another skill, and that's what I call *The Courage to Know When*.

Knowing "When"

As a marketer, I have been classically trained to work with the Five Ws: Who, What, When, Where, and Why. *Who* is the target audience, *What* do you want to sell them, *When* do you want to sell them, *Where* do you want to sell them, and *Why* they want what you have. Of all the Five Ws, I'm going to focus on the **When**. Because **When** is the point that you have to make the decision to *act*. All the other Ws involve research, analysis, projections, and plans. But there always comes a moment when you've got to flip the switch to on. And that is what takes *courage*.

Whether it's a career move, a business idea, or a relationship, you've got to make the decision to act. Now, you're probably thinking that means you have to make a decision to move forward. Sometimes yes, sometimes no. The courage to know **When** involves knowing when to go forward and when to stand still. When to be strong and when to be vulnerable. When to know your stuff, and when to know what you don't know, so that you are open to good advice. When to speak, and when to be quiet—and let silence or the door closing behind you speak for you. But always, always, at key points, you have to exercise *The Courage to Know When.*

Sometimes in business and in life you don't get what you want. But this situation with CPS was different. I could tell the reason we weren't getting more business was based on biases, to my being a woman, and being a woman of color. Other vendors of color had experienced issues with this purchasing manager, and his dismissive attitude was obvious. The elephant in the room could not hide. Sometimes you have to have the courage to know when it's time to leave the room.

Was I scared? Absolutely. But I could not let fear stop me. This was our biggest customer, and I was a single mother with two kids to put through school. I knew what had happened was wrong. I documented carefully and objectively everything we had done to gain and maintain the CPS business over time, outlining the cost savings for them and volumes involved. As mentioned, I had worked hard to have good relations with CPS for years, and I also had good relations with key members in the community for support.

And guess what happened? I Pivoted to Maintaining Perseverance and won. We got our increase in volume, the purchasing manager no longer worked for CPS, and bounce-backability kicked in big time.

In your experience in life or as an entrepreneur, your moments of Maintaining Perseverance may not be as dramatic as what happened to us at CPS. But Maintaining Perseverance will be as important to your business just the same. For example, in the early days of starting The Hilliard Group in 1995, I ordered a new computer system from Dell Computer. I had been impressed with their new advertisements about how they were there for small business own-ers, and that resonated with me. After my new computer arrived, things were humming right along, but then I'd have glitches in my system. Whenever I'd call customer support, I had a lot of trouble getting someone on the phone. I knew Dell was growing by leaps and bounds at that time and adjusting their business and customer service models. Still, it was very frustrating for me. It would take a long time to get to the right area of customer or technical support, and then I had to get the right technician who would try to solve my problem.

The glitches started getting worse, and one day my system crashed altogether. I couldn't get anyone live on the phone to help me. I even called Michael Dell's office! They were very understand-ing and said they would have someone call me to help. Well, my entire business was on that computer, I had a major presentation to send out, and I was increasingly frantic about what to do. (Full transparency: it has taken me years to employ Having Patience with technology glitches. I'm much better now.)

In true Pivot-style of Maintaining Perseverance, I identified my options. The best one I had and the most accessible one in real time was to call on the neighborhood computer genius, who happened to be my best friend's son, who was about nine years old at the time. I kid you not. Jason Smikle is the son of Renee Ferguson and Ken Smikle, and it was at their Christmas table where the Comfort-Cake name was born. By the time Jason was in fourth grade, he was already taking computers apart and putting them back together. I called his mom and told her that she had to send him over imme-diately. Jason came over, and quietly started to look over my com-puter. I had to leave the room to not hover nervously. I don't know what he did, but about an hour or so later, I was back in business! Jason saved my company! To this day, we laugh about it.

Today, Jason and his partner, Ebele Mora, a Nigerian immi-grant, own a major global digital market research company. I'm not surprised, given his genius at nine years old. I trusted Jason's abilities (then and now). When Maintaining Perseverance, go with your gut. It knows. And by the way, Michael Dell's office did call back, and they replaced my system in a few days.

An important key in Maintaining Perseverance is knowing how long to persevere. Part of that knowing is determining whether it is the right time or the right circumstance for what you are trying to make happen in your business or life. Sometimes you will not know this until you are in the thick of the Pivot of Maintaining Perseverance.

We experienced this when ComfortCake was invited to appear on Home Shopping Network. As a fan of HSN, I always enjoyed watching the segments and seeing the numbers of customer orders and sales keep growing as the spokesperson engaged with the product spokesperson as they discussed how the products were made and how to use them, what they tasted like, and what incredible deals consumers could get.

To get on the show, I first went the traditional route through the HSN website and got no response. Then a friend introduced me to a marketing impresario who knew the head of HSN. Next thing I knew, we were in the marketing guru's office, and he had the head of HSN on the phone. He said, "There's this pound cake company you should see. Tastes great. You'll see them? Terrific. I'll have them call your office." Sometimes, that's how things happen. One phone call, and you're in. But that was just the start.

We were slated to be on HSN in the winter of 2006—Christmas season. There was a lot to learn before you go on camera. After all, HSN is successful for a reason—they know what they are doing and teach you how to do it. First, we had to go their headquarters in St. Petersburg, Florida, to what I call HSN University. We learned food presentation, scripts, timing, camera angles, wardrobe—everything. Then, at the same time, your products had to be approved—and that meant quality, packaging, pricing, frozen warehousing, distribution, and shipping. Shipping was tantamount. Orders had to be shipped to customers within 48 hours of being placed on the show.

We learned well, and our segment was a hit. Seeing those numbers tally up was so exciting! But then, when we got back to our office in Chicago, after being in Florida, it was bitterly cold. And those orders had to shipped. We arranged for the UPS trucks to come in shifts, as fast as we could print labels and slap them on the boxes of Bundt cakes. There was just our small staff of three handling over 700 cakes going out, and we could barely keep up. It got so bad that the UPS guys helped us by putting the shipping labels on. Working as a team, we got it done. Whew!

HSN was pleased with our performance and invited us back. We included mini Bundts and slices, as well as Sugarless Sweetness versions, on our next segment. The Sugarless Sweetness versions sold out the fastest. And we got those orders out on time also. We Maintained Perseverance to perform well, and HSN wanted us to come back yet again. That was when I had to stop and assess if this was the right business model for ComfortCake. Many of HSN's suppliers only supply HSN. It can do that kind of business for a company. However, operationally, it is a very large commitment, and I had other distribution channels to service. Also, during this time, I had been seeking more capital to help us grow, which was challenging, as was hiring more experienced food executives to work in a start-up environment. It was not time to change the business over to an HSN-driven distribution business. The volume was good, but it did not match the foodservice volume and profits we were making from our other clients. So, I decided not to persevere any longer, and it was the right decision for The ComfortCake Company.

Lesson: You can Pivot to Maintaining Perseverance for a long time, but you must be sure it is the best path to follow given your Defined Priorities and resources.

Synergies Pay Off

Finally, the Pivots of Maintaining Perseverance and Having Patience (#6) have a lot in common. They are synergistic in that you can Hone Your Vision and Shift Your Energy, yet to Make Your Move and have it pan out takes both Patience (waiting for the right time) and Perseverance (not giving up). This happened for me with McDonald's. As mentioned in Having Patience, I first approached McDonald's in 2002 about getting ComfortCake on their menus. We weren't able to get a test until 2009, seven years later. I can't share many details, but here is what I can share with you about how that happened.

After being put in touch with the consulting firm that handled new product development for McDonald's, and presenting our product and information, we were turned down due to other menu priorities. However, I kept in touch with everyone I met along the way. For years, on every road trip with my kids, we'd always stop at McDonald's. I'd take the time to ask the counter servers if they thought a pound cake would do well there and take note of their responses. At the Essence Music Festival in New Orleans, McDonald's was a major sponsor. A former client from The Hilliard Group was also a sponsor and invited me to attend. There I met other key McDonald's people. I always traveled with ComfortCake slices on hand to show our capabilities and got positive taste responses many times. The purpose of these interactions was to network with key executives and stay in the game. I had no idea when, if ever, McDonald's might be interested in a pound cake. At a community event in Chicago, I had the opportunity to meet Magic Johnson, who at the time owned several Starbucks stores. I had pitched Starbucks a few years earlier, and they were interested in ComfortCake; however, the timing didn't work out for us in their purchasing cycles. What I did learn, however, is how popular pound cake was with coffee. I also knew this from selling ComfortCake at 7-Eleven stores. When I met Magic Johnson, I asked him personally how pound cake sold for him at Starbucks. He said it was a real winner. I kept this information in my files.

Did I also try to sell other fast-food restaurant companies? Of course. But as a small company, I had Defined My Priorities (#3), and pursuing companies headquartered locally (McDonald's was headquartered in Oakbrook, a suburb of Chicago) kept me closer to my family. I just kept Pivoting to Having Patience and Maintaining Perseverance in gaining information and networking to develop relationships that could be helpful. In particular, we maintained good relationships with the Black owner-operators of McDonald's franchises and supported their fundraising efforts to the community. Supporting the community is a shared value between McDonald's and our company as well. By keeping up with the strategic priorities of McDonald's and maintaining good relationships, seven years later when they were ready to test pound cakes, we were invited to participate. ComfortCake's Lemon Pound Cake ended up being in a 50-store market test in three cities. It was a major step forward from my kitchen to being tested and approved to become a McDonald's supplier. To this day, I continue to Have Patience and Pivot to Maintaining Perseverance as I adjust my business models for the Defined Priorities that have evolved for my life. Let's see what the future may hold!

PIVOT

Maintaining Perseverance Takes Managing Your Perspectives

The pursuit of your passions and purpose is a journey—twists and turns are guaranteed. To get where you want to go, you must Have Patience, but also you must Pivot and Maintain Perseverance so that at the right time, in the right circumstances, and when everything aligns, you are ready to execute your plan and realize your dream.

Here are the key lessons from Maintaining Perseverance:

- You have to decide you will keep going but, over time, continue to assess if it is right to keep going.

- Bounce-backability is both a mindset and a skill set. First, you must decide to do it, then find creative ways to do so.
- Seeking Positivity, Defining Priorities, and knowing your value and networking are important facets of Maintaining Perseverance.
- The Courage to Know When and how to act is vital.
- Maintaining Perseverance and Having Patience are key synergistic pivots that can work in your favor.

10

Managing Perceptions

There's no such thing as a second first impression.

WHEN I WAS growing up as one of four daughters, I noticed how my mother had to learn how to be creative to present us to the world as she wanted us to be seen. Both my parents came from working-class backgrounds and worked hard to better themselves in life. My mother was a nurse who went to college at night *after* she had all of us to become a teacher, and my father became a medical technician when he couldn't afford to go to medical school. They both always worked and wanted the best for us.

A stylish but savvy woman, my mother could sew, so she made outfits for us. But it was her savvy that was truly creative. She would take us shopping at the best department stores in Detroit to look at the high-quality clothes when they first arrived in the store. Then she would take us back when they went on sale. Not the first markdowns, not the second, but the final markdowns, when they went to the clearance basements. My mother was the queen of the

145

clearance racks. No one shopped them better, and she made the most of the resources my parents could afford. She knew quality, and we always looked like quality as we represented our family. It was a skill I learned from her, and it has come in handy all my life to Manage Perceptions.

How You Present Yourself Impacts Your Potential for Success

We were taught from a young age the importance of presenting ourselves well. It would help you get into good schools, get good jobs, and have many other positive opportunities. How you walked, talked, and interacted with people was nothing to take lightly, or shoot from the hip. We were lucky to have parents with that foresight and mindset, though at times it could seem rather strict. As I matured, however, I learned from multiple experiences and remembrances just how powerful the pivot of Managing Perceptions is.

One such experience occurred when I was about seven years old and it is seared in my memory. As African Americans, traveling across the country in the 1950s and 60s could be perilous. About 1959, we were taking the train to Los Angeles to visit Mom's sister and her family. To me, it was an exciting trip. We had packed a lot of food to bring with us, as Mom knew that we may not be able to be served everywhere we stopped. By the time we got to a stop in Texas, we needed to buy sandwiches. We were well dressed for our trip; hair done with bows, shirts neatly tucked in. Mom wore a plain, belted black jumpsuit that I always thought made her look like a movie star. We went up to the lunch counter to order sandwiches, and sat down in the tall swivel chairs. The waitress quickly came over to us and took our order. She brought it over promptly but said dismissively, "Here's your order, but y'all can't eat it at this counter."

I was so surprised; there were plenty of seats. This hadn't happened to us in Detroit. It was my first experience of discrimination. I so clearly remember Mom squaring her shoulders, standing up tall, looking regal in that jumpsuit, and calmly telling the waitress in no uncertain terms that, "We have train tickets like everyone else here. We have paid for our sandwiches with money like everyone else here, and we intend to eat them at this counter like everyone else here." The perception that Mom managed was unequivocable.

Now, I don't know what the laws were in that Texas train station, so perhaps the waitress was bluffing. Perhaps Mom was tired after traveling with children. But she wasn't having it. Mom looked like, talked like, and managed the total perception that she meant business. She sat down, and we had a very nice lunch.

This experience came to mind many years later in 1974 on my new job as the assistant buyer at Bloomingdale's when, as I related in Pivot Point #6, Having Patience, I was told, "Deliveries are in the back" when I arrived early at the Halston fashion show to get seats for my buyer and myself. The vision of my mother's presence at that Texas lunch counter came back full force. I knew I had to present myself well to Manage the Perception that I belonged at that Halston show and belonged in the front row.

As you Hone Your Vision, Shift Your Energy, and Make Your Move, it is critical you master this final Pivot Point. As the saying goes, perception is reality. If you want to do well in school, you have to manage how your teachers or professors perceive your performance. This was true for me in my Harvard Business School marketing class with Professor Steve Starr. As I shared in Pivot Point #5, Getting Prepared, I had to manage the perception he and my classmates had of me: that I knew what I was talking about as I was called on to present a case study. In business, you must Manage Perceptions with colleagues, your boss, and your team to get ahead. I got some great advice from a mentor at Gillette about this. When you are writing a memo or a proposal, or making a presentation, do it in a way that your audience keeps nodding their heads in the meeting or as they read what you wrote. Don't put in jarring information that throws them off your flow. I never forgot this tip—and trust me—it works every time in Managing Perceptions. If you keep it in mind as you develop your work, it becomes a habit.

Companies must present their products, services, and business practices well to customers. I spent years in advertising, and presenting companies well is the job of that profession. However, there are other aspects of Managing Perceptions that are important in business and can have an impact on both the bottom line and shareholder value. Customer service is one of them. According to mediapost.com, US businesses annually lose $83 billion due to poor customer service.[1] If treated poorly, 56% of customers polled will never use a company again, and 20% will spread the word about their poor experience on social media. Companies like Southwest Airlines, Disney, and Trader Joe's are known for their positive customer service experiences at all levels of their corporations and they value consumers' perceptions very highly.

As an aside, even personally, parents have to manage the perceptions of what their children think of them. As a single mother, I remember it was important to let my son know I meant business when he was a young boy and had to look up to me, so that when he got to be over six feet tall and I had to look up to him, he still believed it!

We've all heard the saying, "dress for success." That is all about Managing Perceptions. While a lot of business attire has become more casual in certain professions, you still need to look the part—as well as act the part—to be taken seriously. You don't want there to be a disconnect in the transmission of what you are saying and the nonverbal communication of what your clothes represent. To have confidence in them, I want my doctor or financial advisor to look like one, not like a member of a rock band. Even if you are in a "business casual" professional environment, keep your radar up on how far you take "casual" as you seek to climb the ladder. You want

---

[1] Jack Loechner, "Poor Customer Service Costs Companies $83 Billion Annually," MediaPost *Research Brief* (Feb. 18, 2010), https://www.mediapost.com/publications/article/122502/poor-customer-service-costs-companies-83-billion.html

to fit into your environment, and still let people know you mean business. There are so many options today to choose from to look pulled together very casually; and if you buy quality, that can send the right message, too.

An important caveat—if you are in sales, especially retail sales, you want to represent what you are selling, but be careful not to assume that the way a *customer* dresses conveys how much money they have to spend. This may not be the case at all. I learned this from my days selling in retail. When I was learning the ropes as a salesperson at a cool boutique to make money while in college, the top seller on the floor always dressed in the newest fashions from the store. She watched customers as they came into the store, observing their body language to gauge their state of mind. Were they confident, shy, in a hurry, or grazing? Sure, some customers confidently walked in wearing the latest fashions and knew what they wanted; yet many of them used layaway. But some came in and shyly walked around because they didn't know what looked best and needed direction—they often had loads of money to spend. The top seller at the boutique could tell, made no judgments about what they wore into the store, but made sure that when they left, their bags were full of new outfits that would represent them well and their heads were held high. I learned from the top seller and became one myself. I loved being able to instill confidence in my customers as I helped them improve their ability to Manage their Perceptions. Retail was a great learning ground.

Don't Advertise What You Don't Have—But Leverage What You Do

Pivoting to Managing Perceptions is not about pretending to be someone you are not or being manipulative. Rather, it is about developing the sense of self of who you want to be and projecting that sense of self in everything the world sees about you as you are making things happen. It is about being consistent in your appearance, words, and deeds. As you Pivot for Success and Find

Your Purpose, Believe in Possibilities, and Honor Your Passion, revisit things that are unique about you. What is your Unique Self Profile—your USP? What talents, gifts, or ways of going about life do you have that can be elevated to manage how others perceive you? This is a key consideration when you are creating or revising your résumé or CV, applying or interviewing for opportunities, or making presentations. I must share a relevant and invaluable piece of advice I learned from Marvin Traub, the CEO of Bloomingdale's.

As I mentioned in Pivot Point #7, Seeking Positivity, I returned to Bloomingdale's after receiving my MBA from Harvard as an associate buyer in the Towel department, the most profitable department in the entire store. Every sales promotion had to be meticulously planned for the best return on investment, or ROI. Each year, there would be two "White Sales," one in fall and one in spring, introducing the new and continuing colors at discounted pricing for a limited time. Each White Sale was announced in full-page color ads in the *New York Times*, showing all the available colors. One season, we ran the White Sale ad and merchandised the selling floor, stacking the towels by color table after table. It was a sea of beautiful, colorful towels. Suddenly, before the store opened, we heard Mr. Traub, the CEO, loudly on our floor calling out "Where is Cerulean Blue? Where is Cerulean Blue? It is not on the floor and it is in the ad! This is unacceptable! Find them!" And he walked away.

The team rushed out to find that the Cerulean Blue towels had not made it from the stockroom to the floor. We had to find them before the store opened its doors. We finally found them in cartons that had been mismarked and rushed to bring them out. Before the opening bell rang, Mr. Traub came back, brought us together, looked at us seriously, and thanked us for fixing the problem. He told us to always remember one thing:

"Don't advertise what you don't have."

And then he turned and walked away. It was advice I carry with me to this day. While he was talking about towels, I realized his words

meant much more. Later, my team and I talked about the importance of his message. Customers will be disappointed. Sales will be
lost. The store's reputation for customer service can be harmed. Trust
can be broken.

This simple axiom I learned in 1978 applies to so much of life.
I have never forgotten it. When you are Managing Perceptions,
don't oversell and underdeliver. Be truthful about your skills, on
your résumé or CV, your website, or what you discuss with prospective employers, clients, or customers. But position them as positively
as you can. Stand tall and look people in the eye when you meet
with them—and project that same confidence when you speak by
phone—so they know your word is good. Look like the goal you are
going after, and present with enthusiasm what you, your team, your
product, and your business can deliver. That way, perception and
reality align.

This brings me to the "fake it 'til you make it" syndrome. We
have all heard that one. It is related to "don't advertise what you
don't have." Often, people are advised to Manage Perceptions by
faking it just enough until they land what they are seeking. For
example, let's say you are going for a global position in your company. You have the core business skills, but you are not bilingual.
You may know enough key phrases in a foreign language to hail a
cab and get a hotel room. But negotiate a business contract? You
can't fake that one. However, you can be authentic and manage the
perception that you can do the job with a good interpreter because
you know the company's products and strategies better than anyone else, and you are willing to learn enough of the language and
cultural nuances to be proficient over time. It's about staying true
to core skills and deliverables you do have, and not faking those.
Trouble happens when you try to be what you aren't or convey skills
or experience you don't have. You will be found out, and that will
undermine all your efforts.

Another example is the advice often given to women that
big business is done on the golf course. I used to believe that, and
bought a set of good golf clubs, a golf travel bag, shoes, golf clothes,

took lessons—the whole bit. I tried hard, but the truth was, I wasn't really good at golf and didn't have the patience for it—and it showed. I ended up selling all that stuff to a woman who was good at golf and enjoyed it as a recreational hobby. And I've done rather well at business anyway.

The key difference is that *you can fake confidence, not competence.* You can be nervous about presenting in a big meeting and feign confidence if you are *competent* about the subject matter at hand. Knowing where you are competent is a big advantage in Pivoting to Managing Perceptions and finding the right approach to "faking it 'til you make it."

Another consideration in Pivoting to Managing Perceptions is going back to your Unique Self Profile (USP) and leveraging what makes you unique to your advantage. You may be different from your colleagues. In the early days of my career, I was often the only African American in the room. I used that to my advantage to provide a different perspective and in doing so found a strategic market gap that Gillette wasn't addressing. In that way I added considerable value to the company and created a new direction for my career. And, by the way, I upped my confidence when presenting to management by always wearing a red suit when I did. I wanted to make sure all eyes were on me. Leveraging what you have can be powerful—in boardrooms and in the marketplace. When attempting to carve a path in a crowded market, defining and leveraging a USP—your Unique Self Profile and in marketing terms, a *Unique Selling Proposition*—can help you Pivot to Managing Perceptions quite effectively, especially when resources may be limited.

When I launched The ComfortCake Company and went after retail distribution, we needed to set ourselves apart. Otherwise, how could we compete against Sara Lee and Entenmann's, the top pound cakes sold in the grocery store channels? I knew we had something they did not—that ComfortCake was made from scratch. I specifically required that our bakeries not use any dried or powdered ingredients for production efficiencies. It was challenging to commercialize my home recipe because of that requirement, but I knew it would make us unique. I also knew that my recipe came from a Southern heritage, as one of my children's grandmothers from North Carolina gave me her "secret tip" for making pound cake super rich in texture. When the bakeries saw it, they told me it wouldn't work. But we scaled up the batches slowly until it did. We were able to position ComfortCake as "the only made-from-scratch, Southern-style pound cake in mass distribution." That was our Unique Selling Proposition. That USP allowed us to Pivot toward a positioning and Perception we could own that was indeed a reality. That's how we competed against much larger companies. It was on all our marketing materials and selling sheets, and it made a big difference in getting us on retail shelves.

Our trademarked slogan also Managed our Perception that we were "in it to win it." To this day, whenever I mention The ComfortCake Company, makers of *"Poundcake So Good It Feels Like a Hug™,"* I get an immediate positive reaction. That slogan opened doors, got us major distribution, investors, publicity. It's part of our legacy. And I hope you caught that it is trademarked as is The ComfortCake® Company. The trademarks communicated our Pivot of Managing Perceptions that we were a company to be taken seriously, and not one to be taken advantage of. The slogans and trademarks are part of our packaging that I spent considerable start-up funds to secure. I strategically wanted our packaging to look like we were already a company that deserved to be on the shelves of national companies. All our selling materials, website, presentation decks, samples, business cards, *everything* that represented The ComfortCake Company were designed specifically to look like we were a national company from day one. It was worth the money to Manage the Perception as we built the business to the million-dollar range.

In Managing Perceptions, I'm a big fan of leveraging what you have. That's why it's worth it to really take stock of what you, your idea, your product, your team, or your business bring to the table. Know your value by doing your research. There may be something you have that the competition doesn't, and it's right in your wheel-house—right within you or your brand. Brand equity can be a big leverage factor. For example, part of the reason I took the job at Fashion Fair was because the cosmetic brand had equity. When I came on as president, the brand hadn't advertised in a while, but women all over the country knew the brand name. That's *leverage and value*. Resources were tight, but with limited advertising, promotions, and e-commerce sales, both loyal and new consumers responded in a very competitive arena and challenging distribution channel. It was still hard competing against the giant cosmetic companies that had finally discovered that women of color are great consumers. As the brand is being revitalized again under new owners to be brought back to the market, the brand name still resonates with women. That's because for years it was the premier cosmetic brand for women of color around the world, and the products had great quality. Mrs. Eunice Johnson created the Fashion Fair touring fashion show in the late 1950s, and it was the "don't miss" event of the year in major cities across the country for decades, raising millions for charity. Many women would love the touring Fashion Fair show to come back; the brand still has that kind of equity power to put into play.

Put Your O.A.R. in the Water

The goal of the Managing Perceptions Pivot is to manage what you can put into action to receive the best possible outcome. For example, become aware of the energy you give out, the situation at hand, the available resources, the emotions and goals of all involved that others would respond to. Part of being successful at Managing Perceptions is knowing how to put your O.A.R. in the water and row to the other side. Let me explain.

Companies spend millions of dollars on focus groups and market research to determine what consumers may decide to purchase or how they will respond to advertising. When you have a big meeting, investor presentation, job interview, or even a closing on your home loan to prepare for, you may not have that kind of information to rely on. Whatever research you have, use it. Either way, you've got to put your O.A.R. in the water and **O**bserve, **A**ssess, and **R**espond. This is not asking you to become Dick Tracy, looking for fingerprints and minute clues before you make a move. It is recommending that you Observe: Research your situation, the data, the key players, the strategic priorities, the preferences, the competition, how much time is available to interact, the pressures, the dynamics, etc., that you'll be dealing with. Observe the same things about *yourself*. Knowing these same parameters about yourself is what can help you manage your emotions as you Pivot to Managing Perceptions. Then Assess. This is the nuance and balance you must learn as you Manage Perceptions.

Learn how to read the room in whatever situation you are in. What is the energy in the environment or surrounding the situation? Tense or relaxed? How are you feeling? Is this the best time to schedule an interaction? Does the room setup align with the objective? Remember, you are *Managing* Perceptions. That means, to the extent possible, you are setting things up for the best possible outcome. It is hard to put your best foot forward when your energy level is low, or you are burned out, or the PowerPoint doesn't work. When presenting, *always* arrive early to check the audiovisual equipment. I am a zealot about that. To put a strong O.A.R. in the water and row successfully to your goal, everything must be in sync and moving in the same direction. By using the O.A.R. approach, you are better positioned to more effectively Respond, instead of reacting to whatever perceptions may come up as you approach you goal.

Understand, there will be situations when you will have ample time to go through this process. And there will be times when you will have to go through this process in minutes. This is why I recommend you get used to thinking of Managing Perceptions as the opportunity to successfully row your boat to the other side. As a situation arises, start thinking: What do I have to do to put that

O.A.R. in the water? **O**bserve. **A**ssess. **R**espond. You can make the time, no matter how busy you are. You can do this while commuting, while making small talk on the trade show floor, or while you are talking with the assistant as you wait for your appointment time. But, please, do not be shallow; people pick up on that like a blip on the radar.

Importantly, keep in mind that a best possible outcome means a positive one for all concerned. Everyone will still be tuned into the station WIFM (What's in It For Me?), on their notepad, laptop, smartphone, or tablet as you are making your case. As Aretha Franklin sang, "Give them something they can *feel*" to best Pivot to Managing Perceptions. And never forget: Seek Positivity. Even in a worst-case scenario, there is a best possible outcome. Have Patience.

As I've made adjustments to my businesses over time, Managing Perceptions has been quite a journey. Most people see me smiling and dressed stylishly and have no idea what it has taken to build a food business from scratch and compete against multibillion-dollar companies. That was by design as my Defined Priorities were to keep things moving and ensure my two children finished college so they would have the opportunities to go for their own dreams. I knew that with my education, my skills, my faith, and my health, I would be able to secure employment if I had to completely shut down The ComfortCake Company. However, that was not what I desired to do. I knew that the intellectual property of the business had value, and it was my goal to wind down the active operations of the company quietly, while keeping the company intact, and move into licensing. It was a strategic decision to pivot into a new way of doing business—and trust me, I used the synergy of all 10 Pivot Points to forge a new path.

To have the best possible outcome, Managing Perceptions was and is important. For me, it was important in that I knew my marketing skills were still very much intact, so The Hilliard Group (THG) would continue serving clients well. It was gratifying when I moved from the condo to go through my files from THG and see the proposals, projects, and other deliverables that have been produced over the years for exemplary corporations and significant nonprofit entities. I am very proud of this work that has helped move multicultural marketing forward and gratified that THG continues after 25 years.

I am also pleased to have come to a place where I can share the full story of The ComfortCake Company, and no longer have to Manage the Perception that everything was smooth sailing, and we didn't have major challenges as we built the business. The Comfort-Cake Company is still proudly here after 19 years!

P↑↓VOT

Managing Perceptions Takes Awareness

The triumphs *and* challenges of The ComfortCake Company are part of my story, and by telling others about this journey I hope to educate people seeking to follow their dreams. Going for your dream can absolutely be one of the most exciting things you can ever do—and can also be one of the most excruciating. The Pivot to Managing the Perception of both is quite a balancing act! Most entrepreneurial stories are primarily about the successes. Sharing both sides of the story is important to create authentic awareness in others about entrepreneurship. A benefit of doing so is the unleashed energy I have as I Maintain Perseverance going forward to my third act, and I'm truly excited about that!

Here are the key lessons from Managing Perceptions:

- How you present yourself has an impact on your potential for success.
- Don't advertise what you don't have—it can undermine your efforts.

- Know your USPs—Unique Self Profiles and Unique Selling Propositions.
- Leverage what you have personally and professionally.
- Put your O.A.R. in the water—**O**bserve. **A**ssess. **R**espond.
- Keep your head up through challenges by relying on the synergies of the 10 Pivot Points.

Epilogue: Pivot for Success

I won a lot by losing Everything.

As YOU COME to the end of this book, you may still be wondering, "If The ComfortCake Company was such a terrific idea, why hasn't Amy been super successful and rich by now? Why didn't she sell the company earlier? Why didn't she . . ."

Let me be very honest with you. I may not be rich, but I am incredibly successful. It is all in how you Envision Prosperity. I always knew I would take ComfortCake as far as I could, and then use my experience to teach others so that someone, somewhere would take things farther than I did. And truth be told, the ComfortCake story is still being written. Trust me on that one. But even if nothing comes to pass, I'm good.

Recently, Phylicia Rashad and Debbie Allen did an Instagram show on their lives as sisters, and what was most gratifying for them. For both, it was teaching. Tony Award–winning actress and director Phylicia Rashad teaches master classes in acting at prestigious universities all over the country. And Debbie Allen teaches dancers of all ages at her Debbie Allen Dance Academy. Both spoke glowingly about the love of seeing the spark of light come on in students' eyes, and I agree. But I didn't get to this place easily.

Beginning in 2018, I experienced two years of significant personal losses for me. First, in May of that year, one of my mentees, Chef Judson Allen, a gifted and talented Food Network star, died suddenly of a heart attack at the age of 38. I read about it on Facebook as I came back in from a walk on the lakefront. I thought it had to be a huge mistake. His death stunned me and the city of Chicago, making many people rethink their lives. He was only 38 years old! Then, in August, Ken Smikle, my best friend Renee's husband of over 30 years and a dear friend, suffered a major heart attack. I was on my way to visit my mom in New York, literally on my way to the airport, when their son Jason called me frantically. He was on his way home to Chicago and pleaded with me to get to the hospital because Renee was there all alone with Ken, who had just been brought in by ambulance. I rushed right over. Paramedics had brought him back to life at the house, and he hung on for about a month, before passing in September 2018. Then, Barry Rand, the former CEO of Avis and former chair of Howard University's board of trustees and wonderful mentor to me, died that November. By this time, my mom was declining fast. We knew Thanksgiving that year might be her last, so we all planned to be in Baltimore as a family. Mom was weak, but she was so very happy we were all there.

On December 10, 2018, my mom died in her sleep. And the foundation of my world shifted.

Losing my last parent was devastating. Because she was a woman, my mother, and my role model, my own mortality came sharply into focus. Her death has been the most powerful Pivot Point of all. I now have an undeniable sense of urgency to Pivot toward the best possible use of the years I have left of this life. Honestly, there were times in the year after her death when grief overwhelmed me, and I couldn't stop crying, couldn't breathe, and couldn't believe she was gone. I've probably sent out emails to potential clients with typos and was just totally off center at times.

In May 2019, I lost another dear friend, Emmett Vaughn, who was 63. A key executive of Exelon Corporation, Emmett was a leader in the field of Supplier Diversity. Known as a champion of not only inclusion but equity, Emmett brought his A-game to this cause and made sure corporations did too. He played a major role in securing over $1.5 billion in contracts for minority suppliers. I was one of them. As an executive with Jewel stores, Emmett helped me secure early retail distribution for ComfortCake in those 25 grocery stores.

Next was Jada Russell: a beautiful public relations and marketing entrepreneur, full of life and joy, always smiling, offering advice. We were models together in a fashion show in the fall of 2018, laughing and sashaying down the runway. Diagnosed with breast cancer at age 45 in April 2019, she kept her illness secret until the end when she died in July 2019. A total shock.

Then Greg Hinton. Another friend who loved life, lived big, and died suddenly. The first Chief of Diversity for the Democratic National Convention. As fellow Leos, we shared a love of good motivational quotes, fun social events, and uplifting our community. He had a 66th birthday party on August 4th. On August 27th he had a massive heart attack and was gone.

In October 2019, I lost my friend and Howard University classmate, Congressman Elijah Cummings. He and his wife, Maya, had joined some of our Thanksgiving family gatherings over the years and he enjoyed some ComfortCake. We also sat proudly at Howard events and graduations. His death rocked me hard.

Dr. Gerri Henderson, my dear friend and marketing mentor at Loyola University, the first Black woman to get a PhD in marketing, who wrote the case study on White Rain Shampoo for the Darden School of Business, died suddenly in November 2019— right before we were to get together for drinks for the holidays. I was in shock when I spoke at her memorial service at Loyola's Quinlan School of Business.

As these losses over 2018 and 2019 mounted one right after another, I really have to thank God that my sister Gloria suggested

I try meditation. It saved me. Meditation focuses on breathing. Learning how to just breathe through things helped me slow down the anxiety that had been bubbling underneath the veneer of "fabulousness" I projected as I was Managing Perceptions during that time. It all came to a head for me, as executor of mom's estate, after going through the process of closing down our family home of 50 years. The house was the primary asset. She always said she didn't have much money to leave us, because our parents had invested in our educations and felt we'd do all right for ourselves. But going through the precious memories in the house and preparing it for sale was traumatic. I was the one who had found the house with mom 50 years earlier.

In June of 2019, thanks to some helpful advice, I was able to get a good cash price on the house; but in the process, my heart rate would jump up to scary levels. My doctor put me on a heart monitor for two weeks. That's when Gloria said, "You have got to learn how to *breathe* and *let go!*"

I realized I had to let go of a lot. My parents were gone. And so were dreams I had for a long and successful marriage. A super-rich business with my life partner at my side, a summer home, frequent international travel, celebrity status with millions of likes on social media . . . *yada, yada, yada.*

Lesson: Life truly is short. We are all going to leave here. The only question worth asking is: What will I have done with the dash between the day I was born and the day I will die? Am I living my true calling?

As I reflected on the personal and professional losses suffered, a key realization started coming into focus:

I Won a Lot by Losing Everything

I realize I have Pivoted for Success because I've made the turn toward Clarity. Perspective. Sanity. Identity.

And turned toward reinvention and my ideal path—Teaching.

Through meditation, prayer, and being still I was able to Pivot toward a path I have thought about for years. Again, I used the Pivot Points, but in a different way. Often, when I gave seminars, I used a Venn diagram to visually reinforce how the Pivot Points work together. It's amazing that what you've taught others, you can use to teach yourself. Finding Your Ideal Path is an evolving lifelong journey. And the beauty of the Pivot Points is that by going through the process, Your Ideal Path will continue to show up. I'm sharing the figure below because it highlights how.

Looking at the Venn diagram, Your Ideal Path is a blend of Finding Your Purpose, Believing in Possibilities, and Honoring Your Passion. By aligning with Defining Your Priorities, Envisioning Prosperity, and Having Patience, you can evolve to where you ideally want to be at any stage of your life. Importantly, once you've done that, you can *sustain* where you are by Getting Prepared, Seeking Positivity, Maintaining Perseverance, and Managing Perceptions.

FINDING YOUR IDEAL PATH

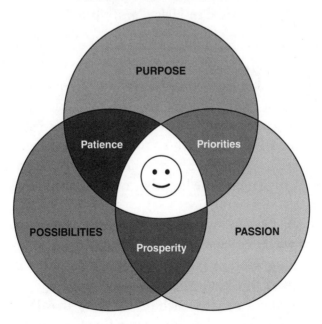

This is another way to use the 10 Pivot Points as you Hone Your Vision, Shift Your Energy, and Make Your Move.

Here's how it works for me in this format:

The Vortex of Purpose, Possibilities, and Passion Provides Powerful Energy, Inspiration, and Gratification

That's *exactly* how I feel in the classroom or when I am speaking to a roomful of people. My students and audiences get a kick out of the stories from my corporate career and my entrepreneurial journey that I mix in with textbook or research-based learning. My hope is that when students leave the classroom, or after others have heard me speak, they will go out into the world and seek opportunities to make people's lives better. It makes me proud to think my work and my experiences will have had something to do with that. When students and audience members let me know they appreciate my approach, it's an awesome feeling.

Defining Your Priorities Can Help Clarify Why

My mom's death changed me. I knew that I wouldn't be here forever, and her death showed me I needed to use my life differently. Mom was a teacher—a dedicated teacher. I remember how she prepared lessons for her classes. She taught science, for example, and I had to feed the snakes and frogs she had in aquariums on our back porch for her students. Yuck! But she wanted to bring real stuff to the classroom. She was no-nonsense, but her passion to make her students be the best they could be came through loud and clear.

When she died, in my grief I had to reflect deeply on what my own legacy would be. Sure, I've had a great career and businesses. But that smiling spot on the Venn diagram was me. I understood why mom loved this honorable profession so much. And though I miss her deeply, she's still teaching me. Now that I've become a teacher myself, I channel her spirit when I stand before my students or an audience. I feel her energy helping me do and say the right things, to challenge them and inspire them at the same time.

Making the decision to teach and to write this book took courage for me. And, I've been asked to bring back ComfortCake. Every day, I get a mention about it. Every. Single. Day. It has been an absolutely wonderful and life-changing journey. After much thought, I know that given the brand equity, the right business model, and a good team, the business could again be substantive. However, a priority in my life is to *grind less and glide more*. So, bringing back ComfortCake can be done, but must be done with that priority in mind.

Having Patience Is Key

'Nuff said. Age is nothing but a number, and it's never too late. At 68 years old, I feel I can teach for many more years in some form or another. Lectures. Online courses. Seminars. Writing. Podcasting. Speaking. It's totally energizing!

Envisioning Prosperity Means Knowing "Your Enough"

Teaching through speaking may not be as lucrative as a corporate career or a big buyout, but I believe it will open doors of income that will more than sustain me. Keeping that smile on my face isn't always about money. In the 18 months *before* the 2020 pandemic, I lost *nine* close loved ones, friends, mentors, and mentees, including my mom. All these deaths rocked me hard but proved to me that money is not everything, and *all money isn't green*. I know that as long as I can look up, I can get up and do the things that truly matter to me. I know that I have my "Enough."

Sustaining Your Ideal Path Matters

This is why Getting Prepared and staying prepared is so important. Preparation will always enable you. Seeking Positivity will help sustain your energy and momentum. Maintaining Perseverance will let bounce-backability kick in when you need it, and Managing Perceptions will let the world know where you are coming from.

As I move forward now, using my gifts, losing my fears, and helping build dreams for others—I know I will be fine, and my dreams will manifest also—with the help of my faith and the 10 Pivot Points. These 10 Pivot Points have never failed me, and I hope they will help you also to:

Hone Your Vision, Shift Your Energy, and Make Your Move

If I can Pivot to Make My Move—at each and every step of the way—then so can you. This is the time.

So, go for it!

Wishing you all the best on your journey!

Acknowledgments

THIS BOOK WOULD not have come into being without the faith, support, and love of the many people in my life who have believed in me and my dreams—and have been there over time to help me see them come to fruition.

First and foremost, I want to thank my parents, Stratford and Gwendolyn Hilliard, for providing me with the love, values, guidance, and trust to not be afraid of trying for the sky. Even when they may not have understood what I was going for, they let me try to do it for the most part, as long as the foundation of my values were intact. I saw them work hard—sometimes working two and three jobs at a time—to support us while staying true to their own ambitions, always prioritizing their love for family and friends, taking pride in their culture, and giving back to their community. While my trying for the sky was encouraged, they did draw the line at my joining the parachute jumping club in college, however!

I am truly thankful for my children, Angelica and Nick, who have been partners with me on my corporate and entrepreneurial journeys, especially ComfortCake. I would not have started ComfortCake without their blessings at 14 and 11 years old, and they have both made substantial contributions to the company. To this day, I continue to rely on their unconditional love, advice, and counsel as they have matured into smart, savvy professionals who I am so proud of. In their own distinctive ways, they have made my heart sing since they were born. Angelica is an advertising executive who consistently gives me her incisive, creative, and often hilarious points of view. Nick is a strategic consultant, and always pushes me to make sure I am looking at all future possibilities. As busy as I became, I never forgot that my first job was being their mom and growing up they made sure I didn't. We always made time for fun and still do.

To my sisters, Pam, Gloria, and Wendy—each entrepreneurs now, growing up together as "The Hilliard Girls" in the city of Detroit was a uniquely wonderful experience. We are all different, and I have learned a lot from each of you. Pam, you are a tenacious teacher, writer, and global consultant—thank you for letting me follow you around growing up, even though I was a pest! Gloria, you have always been an effervescent force of energy that now leads thousands as #1 in Mary Kay. Thank you for keeping me laughing and learning through tough times. Wendy, watching you train as an athlete and break barriers to compete internationally in Rhythmic Gymnastics, and then start a foundation to train thousands of youth, has been awesome. Sisters, doing all this as you raised your families has inspired me to the hills.

I have attempted to get a version of this book published at least three times over many years. I must thank Patricia Crisafulli, an accomplished writer and editor whom I met 10 years ago at a business breakfast while we sat in the green room comparing shoes waiting for our panels to start, for sending my proposal to her contact at Wiley, Editor Jeanenne Ray. I am most grateful to Jeanenne for very quickly seeing the opportunity to help others by sharing my story and bringing me on board. Editorial Assistant Sally Baker added her expert coordinating skills to the process, and Julie Kerr was exceptional as my development editor providing me with direction while keeping up with my ferocious writing pace as our deadlines loomed, and letting my voice come through. The entire Wiley team—especially the graphics department, who did a great job on the book cover—were terrific to work with, including Managing Editor Dawn Kilgore, who guided me through the production process, and Donna J. Weinson, copyeditor.

I am blessed to have dear friends like Renee Ferguson, an award-winning journalist who has encouraged me for years to tell my story to inspire others. She should, as she is part of it—I named Comfort-Cake at her dining room table! Like my dear friend Tricia, Renee willingly read drafts and gave me her valuable insights and edits. Other friends and authors Caroline Clarke, Valerie Graves, and Moe Ross were so supportive as I made my way through the path to writer-land. And Linda Hope, Lydia Griffin, Pepper Miller and Jerri DeVard—I am indebted to you for being there through so much of it—the ups and downs of my life that are in this book. Thank you.

To the staff and supporters of The ComfortCake Company and The Hilliard Group—Claudine Jordan, Cj, of course, who was there from the beginning—and everyone who helped us build two businesses to be very proud of, thank you. Michelle Hoskins, Paul Fregia, Steve Rogers, and Marc Shulman, thanks so much for your early and invaluable advice. To Tom Burrell, my former boss, first THG client, mentor, and friend, you have always inspired me. To all the clients of The Hilliard Group, thank you for your confidence in me. Monique Brinkman-Hill, that first ComfortCake loan was so important! To my ComfortCake advisory board: Eric McKissack, Ralph Moore, Dave Moore, Bob Kallen, and Donna Stein, your guidance was both helpful and encouraging. To ComfortCake investors Valerie Mosley, John and Victoria Rogers, Naomi Henderson, Cheryl Bryson, and supporters Earl Graves Sr., Linda Johnson Rice, Michelle Collins, Cheryl McKissack, Sandra Rand, and Mike Hall, I am supremely grateful and couldn't have done it without any of you. What a journey!

Reverend Jesse Jackson, thank you for your support all these years. I'm so glad you've been there for ComfortCake and I haven't minded making you a special one at all. Indra Nooyi, John Compton, and Steven Williams, thank you for the opportunity to work with your teams on opportunities. To all the McDonald's executives, owner-operators, and team members, it has been an awesome experience working with you—thank you for taking a chance on my home recipe. Terrez Thompson, Rosalind Brewer, Michael Byron, Bob Bloomer, Jean Crudup, Tim Williams, Michelle Hunt, Kimberly Williams, Jim Seidler, Doug Cygan, and Ken Cruikshank: thank you all for championing ComfortCake or Sugarless Sweetness at your companies—it has meant so much.

Ann Fudge, Paula Sneed, and Linda Keene you were my role models of marketing when we were students at Harvard Business School and beyond. You are my brand management divas—I wouldn't be in marketing today if it weren't for the three of you. Linda, you were my boss twice—at Gillette and Pillsbury—but you have always been my friend first, and that is so rare. All of you taught me how to succeed in corporate America, as women and as women of color. Making no apologies for your brilliance and taking no prisoners with your kindness. I was blessed to see what I could be. Susan Taylor, thank you for your friendship and support as I was climbing the marketing ranks in corporate and beyond.

I cannot begin to share how much it has meant to know that, as I relived the stories of building my career and entrepreneurial journeys, relationships that began over 40 years ago and some even earlier are still in place today as I pivoted to different pathways that I never could have imagined. And relationships that began much more recently feel just as important in many significant ways. I am stronger because of everything I've gone through and look forward to continuing to go through life with strength because of you.

About the Author

AMY S. HILLIARD is an award-winning serial entrepreneur. An honors graduate of both Howard University and the Harvard Business School, Amy is a former retailing, senior marketing, and advertising executive with Bloomingdale's, Gillette, Pillsbury, Burrell Communications, and L'Oréal. The Hilliard Group, her strategic marketing consulting firm, has worked with Fortune 500 clients and nonprofits since 1995. In 2001, she founded The ComfortCake® Company—makers of "*Pound Cake So Good It Feels Like a Hug*™"— which gained national distribution with United Airlines, Walmart, and Home Shopping Network, and became an approved supplier to McDonald's. The Company also owns Sugarless Sweetness®, a patent-pending sugar substitute. Amy's marketing innovations were documented in a case study for the University of Virginia's Darden Business School, and she has also taught Marketing at Loyola University's Quinlan School of Business.

A proven thought leader on entrepreneurship, empowerment, and marketing, Amy has been profiled in *Fortune, Success, Entrepreneur, Black Enterprise, Essence,* and *Ebony* and on CNN and NPR. Her blog, *Sizzling After 60—Thriving at Every Stage of Your Life,* is popular among all ages (www.sizzlingafter60.com).

Based in Chicago and passionate about her community and health/wellness, Amy is the proud mother of two young professionals, Angelica and Nick. Amy served two terms as a Trustee of Howard University, 13 years on PepsiCo's Multicultural Advisory Board, and currently sits on the LeanIn.org Advisory Board with Sheryl Sandberg.

Index